PRONTO!
LET'S COOK ITALIAN IN
20
minutes

GINO
D'ACAMPO

GINO D'ACAMPO is one of the UK's most popular TV chefs, having made countless appearances on most leading cookery programmes over the last ten years. In 2009 he was the winner of ITV's hit series *I'm A Celebrity – Get Me Out Of Here!* He has gone on to host five seasons of *Let's Do Lunch – with Gino and Mel*, as well as his own primetime series, *Gino's Italian Escape*. He also appears regularly on ITV's flagship programme, *This Morning*.

Gino is the author of several bestselling cookbooks, including *Fantastico!* – which won the Gourmand Cookbook Award for Best Italian Cookbook in the World – *Buonissimo, Gino's Pasta, The Italian Diet, Italian Home Baking* and *La Dolce Diet*. Recently he opened his first food establishment, My Pasta Bar, in Central London.

To all my Twitter and Facebook followers for all your support over the years

 facebook.com/ginodacampo

 @ginofantastico

First published in Great Britain in 2014
by Kyle Books
an imprint of Kyle Cathie Limited
192–198 Vauxhall Bridge Road
London SW1V 1DX
general.enquiries@kylebooks.com
www.kylebooks.com

10 9 8 7 6 5 4

ISBN: 978 0 85783 102 6

A CIP catalogue record for this title is available from
the British Library

Text © Gino D'Acampo 2014
Photographs © Matt Russell 2014
Design © Kyle Books 2014

Editor: Vicky Orchard
Design: Nicky Collings
Photography: Matt Russell
Food Styling: Gee Charman
Props Styling: Jo Harris
Production: David Hearn and Nic Jones

Colour reproduction by ALTA London
Printed and bound in China by C&C Offset Printing
Company Ltd

CONTENTS

INTRODUCTION

My grandfather (nonno Giovanni) always used to say to me that a great cook should spend more time getting the right ingredients than spending hours in the kitchen trying to prepare a tasty meal. Cooking a good Italian recipe should be quick and easy and – with the right ingredients and equipment – everybody can do it. Millions of you have bought my cookery books in the past 10 years, and I thank you from the bottom of my heart, but lately I have had lots of requests for fast and tasty recipes and I feel it is my responsibility as a cook to push myself and give you what you need: quick, tasty and affordable recipes that anyone can give a go, even during the working week when we're all tired and want food… fast!

When it comes to cooking, the excuse that everybody makes is: I'm too busy. Well, that goes for just about all of us and I understand that with today's hectic lifestyles there never seem to be enough hours in the day BUT we still need to eat. In this book, I am going to show you how to create something fantastic in just 20 minutes that won't overstretch the weekly food budget and that you, your family and friends will love to share and enjoy eating again and again. Let's be honest, it will take you 20 minutes to warm up a ready-meal in the oven or pick up a takeaway, so there's no excuse – just get on with it! Use my 'Italian in 20 minutes' as a frame of mind; when you enter the kitchen relax, put on a bit of music and, if you fancy, have a little glass of wine to make the experience more enjoyable. The first couple of times you cook my recipes it might take you a little longer, but don't worry, remember this is not a competition.

TOOLS
of the
TRADE

- hand blender · food processor
- kettle · microwave · griddle pan
- frying pans (small, medium, large)
- baking trays (small, medium, large)
- lidded saucepans (small, medium, large) · large chopping (cook's) knife
- small peeling knife · long, thin-bladed knife · bread knife · a nice chunky wooden chopping board
- measuring jugs · mixing bowls (small, medium, large) · sieve
- colander · pastry brush

- wooden spoons · tongs
- spatula · fish slice · slotted spoon
- potato masher · potato peeler
- scales · tin opener · box grater
- rolling pin · meat hammer
- large serving plates and bowls

The key to cooking at speed is good organisation. The first thing you need to sort out is your equipment: go round your kitchen and pull out all the utensils you have in your cupboards and ask yourself: how many times have I used this? I am sure you will come across lots of fancy kitchen gadgets that you probably use only once a year. Get rid of them or store them out of your way. To be able to cook my 20-minute recipes you need only the items listed opposite.

As with ingredients, I think it's worth spending a little more and getting something that is good quality: it will cook better and last longer. If you are buying a new set of frying pans, make sure you invest in non-stick ones; they're infinitely easier to cook in and to clean afterwards. Always be careful not to use metal spoons in non-stick frying pans otherwise they will scratch and lose the non-stick coating. I suggest using wooden spoons or plastic-coated spatulas (the silicone ones are great). It is really important to keep your knives in good condition. The biggest mistake that people make is never to sharpen their knives. A good sharp knife will help you to slice and chop quicker instead of wasting lots of time with a blunt one. If you can stretch your budget I would suggest to buying a good knife steel sharpener. Also, tools such as vegetable peelers and graters become blunt with use – it's worth replacing these as soon you notice they are not doing their job.

INGREDIENTS
in your
CUPBOARD

Getting the right ingredients is a must, especially when it comes to store cupboard items, so I have created a very simple list of things you should always have in your cupboard.

-Tinned Ingredients-

chopped tomatoes, plum tomatoes, cherry tomatoes, tomato concentrate, chickpeas, cannellini beans, red kidney beans, borlotti beans, butter beans, anchovy fillets in oil, tuna chunks in oil and pineapple chunks

-Jarred Ingredients-

sun-dried tomatoes in oil, roasted peppers in oil, artichokes hearts in oil, salted capers, English mustard, wholegrain mustard, runny honey, Nutella chocolate spread, strawberry jam and mayonnaise

-Bottled Ingredients-

extra virgin olive oil, olive oil, balsamic vinegar, balsamic glaze, passata, white wine vinegar, red wine vinegar and tomato ketchup

-Dried Pasta and Rice-

penne rigate, rigatoni, spaghetti, linguine, farfalle, fusilli, conchigliette (small shells), orecchiette, short grain (Arborio or risotto) rice, long grain (basmati) rice, microwaveable rice, couscous, bulgar wheat and ready-made polenta

-Baking Ingredients-

plain flour, self-raising flour, cornflour, cocoa powder, baking powder, caster sugar, brown sugar and vanilla extract

-Herbs and Spices-

I am not a big fan of dried herbs or spices; I strongly believe that fresh herbs are much better in flavour and texture but there are a few I find very useful and good in taste: dried oregano, dried chilli flakes, cayenne pepper, smoked paprika, fennel seeds, saffron and nutmeg

-Miscellaneous-

chicken/vegetable/beef stock powder, almonds, hazelnuts, walnuts, pine nuts, pistachio nuts, toasted fine breadcrumbs and dried porcini mushrooms and fresh eggs.

To cook quick but super tasty Italian dishes also requires you to organise your fresh ingredients in the fridge. When reading my recipes you will find that I often use the following fresh ingredients and they are therefore part of my weekly shopping list: eggs, mozzarella balls, block of Parmesan cheese, tub of mascarpone cheese, salted butter, cooked ham, Parma ham, sliced salami, diced pancetta, fresh egg tagliatelle, lasagne sheets, cherry tomatoes, rocket leaves, double cream, creme fraîche and full-fat milk.

SHORTCUTS

to make your

LIFE EASIER AROUND THE KITCHEN

Chopping and slicing ingredients is where everyone wastes the most time when preparing a recipe. Here are a few things you can do to make your life a little easier:

• Finely slice or chop your onions, roll in clingfilm and freeze. They will last frozen for up to 2 months and you can use them straight from the freezer.

• Slice or chop your garlic and put in a clean jam jar. Cover with olive oil and refrigerate. It will last for 10 days.

• Remember you can always prepare ahead big batches of onions and garlic by chopping and slicing using a food processor.

When cooking Italian food fresh herbs are a must; nowadays you can buy those beautiful little growing plants that you can easily keep on your windowsill and they last for weeks. Basil, flatleaf parsley, rosemary and chives are very easy to look after and remember, especially if you have a supply in your garden or allotment, that you can always pick off the leaves, roll them in clingfilm and freeze them ready to be used straight from the freezer. Chop fresh herbs on a large chopping board and use the biggest knife you have to make the job faster.

Once a week, collect all your stale bread and cut into small chunks. Put on a baking tray and cook in the oven at 110°C/gas 1 for 2 hours. Turn off the heat and leave the bread to cool down in the oven. Blitz in a food processor until you have fine crumbs with a sand-like texture. Store in an airtight container for 1 month.

Make up a big batch of tomato sauce, allow it to cool to room temperature, pour it into containers, seal and freeze for up to 2 months. Please defrost before using.

GINO'S TOP TIPS

to become

FASTER AND MORE CONFIDENT

-1-
Pour yourself a glass of wine.

-2-
Switch on the music; I find Dean Martin always helps!

-3-
Before you start, read and understand the recipe, what equipment you will need and what ingredients. You'll get a good idea of what you need to do when and won't have to waste lots of time referring back to the recipe when you could be chopping or cooking.

-4-
Arrange your equipment and ingredients to hand around the working space.

-5-
Don't forget to sip the wine from time to time.

-6-
Make room around you: get kids' toys, magazines, bills, etc. out of the way; only cooking equipment should be on your work surface.

-7-
Clean and clear up as you go along.

-8-
Don't have an argument with your partner: a sad cook doesn't produce good food.

-9-
Don't rush things, 20 minutes is plenty of time to make a good dish. If you feel hurried you are more likely to make a mistake and may have to start again.

-10-
Use local ingredients that are in season, they will be fresher and therefore require less cooking or marinating time.

SOUPS & SMALL PLATES

Zuppe e piatti piccoli

This chapter is full of dishes great for a light dinner, lunch or even for a starter if you're having a dinner party. People often think that soups take a long time to cook but my fast recipes included here preserve the freshness and flavour of the ingredients.

Italian classics such as Carpaccio and bruschetta are easy to make in 20 minutes and perfect dishes if you are pushed for time. These simple recipes require only a handful of ingredients but it's this simplicity that makes them so timeless.

SPEEDY VEGETABLE

and

CANNELLINI BEAN SOUP

Some soups taste best if they're allowed to bubble away long and slow, but this one, with its super-fast cooking time, allows you to preserve the freshness of the vegetables. There isn't actually a set recipe for minestrone, the classic Italian soup – its pedigree goes back to the times before the Romans – as it's usually made using whatever vegetables are in season, but it almost always contains beans, pasta or rice. I've chosen cannellini beans as they are full of flavour, incredibly good for you and one of my favourite pulses.

Minestrone velocissimo

serves 6

6 tablespoons extra virgin olive oil
1 red onion, roughly chopped
2 large carrots, peeled and cut into 1cm cubes
2 celery stalks, washed and cut into 1cm cubes
150g curly Savoy cabbage, roughly chopped
1.5 litres hot vegetable stock
6 slices of rustic country-style bread
1 garlic clove, peeled
1 x 400g can cannellini beans, drained and rinsed
4 tablespoons chopped flatleaf parsley
100g freshly grated Parmesan cheese
Salt and white pepper, to taste

1 Preheat a griddle pan.

2 Heat the oil in a large saucepan and fry the onion, carrots, celery and cabbage for 3 minutes. Stir occasionally with a wooden spoon. Pour in the vegetable stock, bring to the boil and cook for 10 minutes. Stir occasionally.

3 Meanwhile, toast the bread on the preheated griddle pan for about 2 minutes on each side until golden and crispy. Immediately lightly rub with the clove of garlic on one side only. Set aside.

4 Reduce the heat under the saucepan to medium and add the beans and parsley to the vegetables. Season with salt and pepper and continue to cook for a further 3 minutes.

5 To serve, place a slice of bread in each serving bowl and pour over the soup. Sprinkle over some Parmesan and serve immediately.

ROASTED RED PEPPER

and

TOMATO SOUP

A friend of mine was complaining that she found it impossible to make a tasty tomato soup. She said that it always came out too watery or lacked flavour. I created this for her; the sweetness of the roasted red peppers adds that little extra something and this soup will leave you feeling satisfied.

Zuppa di pomodori e peperoni

serves 4

3 tablespoons extra virgin olive oil, plus extra for drizzling
1 medium red onion, peeled and roughly chopped
6 large ripe plum tomatoes, roughly chopped
600ml hot vegetable stock
10 basil leaves, plus extra to garnish
200g roasted red peppers in brine, drained and roughly chopped
Double cream, for drizzling
Salt and white pepper, to taste

1   Heat the oil in a medium saucepan and fry the onion over a medium heat for 2 minutes. Stir occasionally with a wooden spoon. Add in the tomatoes and continue to cook for a further 2 minutes. Keep stirring.

2   Pour in the vegetable stock, add the basil leaves and chopped, roasted peppers and bring to the boil. Reduce the heat and simmer for 10 minutes. Stir occasionally.

3   Remove the saucepan from the heat and use a hand blender to blitz into a smooth soup.

4   Season with salt and pepper and serve in warmed bowls, garnished with a few basil leaves, a drizzle of cream and some extra virgin olive oil. I like to serve this with Italian breadsticks on the side.

PUMPKIN

and

SUN-DRIED TOMATO SOUP

I come up with a new pumpkin recipe every Halloween. I refuse to make faces out of the tough shell and not use the lovely squash itself. Pumpkins are really versatile – they give us oil, seeds and delicious-tasting flesh. There are many different squashes that you could also use for this soup at different times of the year but, come autumn, it's hard to resist buying the huge, smooth, slightly ribbed orange pumpkins that you see everywhere.

Zuppa di zucca e pomodori secchi

serves 4

50g salted butter
500g pumpkin flesh, cut into 1cm cubes
2 celery stalks, roughly chopped
2 garlic cloves, peeled and chopped
100g sun-dried tomatoes in oil, drained and roughly chopped
800ml hot vegetable stock
200ml double cream
2 tablespoons pumpkin seeds
Salt and black pepper, to taste

1 Melt the butter in a large saucepan over a medium heat and fry the pumpkin, celery and garlic for 2 minutes. Stir occasionally with a wooden spoon. Add the sun-dried tomatoes and continue to cook for a further 2 minutes. Keep stirring.

2 Pour in the stock and bring to the boil. Reduce the heat and simmer for 12 minutes. Stir occasionally.

3 Remove the saucepan from the heat and use a hand blender to blitz into a smooth, creamy soup.

4 Pour in the cream, season with salt and pepper and heat through without boiling.

5 Serve in warmed bowls, garnished with pumpkin seeds. Perfect with warm ciabatta.

COLD SUMMER TOMATO SOUP

My children still don't understand why you would choose to have cold soup and yet every time I make this recipe, they are the first to finish. It's one of those unusual recipes that you are just not sure about until you try it. Why give up soup during the warm months? The flavours of these quintessentially Mediterranean ingredients are amazing as they haven't been boiled away, the amount of goodness in one bowl is incredible and its vibrant colour looks great.

Passata fredda di pomodori

serves 6

1 yellow pepper, deseeded
and roughly chopped
1 red pepper, deseeded
and roughly chopped
½ cucumber, roughly chopped
1 medium red onion, peeled
and finely chopped
1 fresh red chilli, deseeded
and roughly chopped
600g ripe plum tomatoes, roughly
chopped
1 x 700ml bottle of passata
2 tablespoons red wine vinegar
2 tablespoons extra virgin
olive oil
10 basil leaves
1 tablespoon caster sugar
Salt and white pepper, to taste

1 Separate out a quarter of the prepared yellow and red pepper, cucumber and red onion. Chop very finely and set aside for the garnish.

2 Put all the remaining ingredients in a blender or food processor and blitz until smooth. You may need to do this in 2 batches.

3 Pass the blitzed soup through a sieve into a large clean bowl, pushing it through with a tablespoon to extract the maximum amount of flavour.

4 Season with salt and pepper and transfer to the fridge to rest for 5 minutes.

5 To serve, ladle into bowls and garnish with the reserved chopped vegetables scattered on top.

FRESH PEA

and

BASIL SOUP

We often have peas in the D'Acampo home and I must admit I created this recipe when I was just about to go on holiday and literally the only thing in my fridge was peas. It was pouring with rain outside and I wanted something warm and comforting. And this is what I created – an amazing pea soup made in minutes. Peas are starchy, which gives great texture to the soup, and they are incredibly high in fibre, protein, vitamins and minerals. Although mint is often paired with peas, basil is what gives the soup its Italian lilt.

Zuppa di pisellini

serves 4

2 tablespoons salted butter
2 tablespoons olive oil
1 medium white onion, peeled
and finely chopped
600g fresh peas, podded weight
600ml boiling water
15 basil leaves
1 vegetable stock cube
100ml double cream, plus a little
extra to garnish
Salt and white pepper, to taste

1 Melt the butter in a large saucepan with the oil and fry the onion over a medium heat for 2 minutes. Stir occasionally with a wooden spoon. Add the peas and continue to cook for a further 2 minutes. Keep stirring.

2 Pour in the water, add the basil leaves and stock cube and bring to the boil. Reduce the heat and simmer for 12 minutes. Stir occasionally.

3 Remove the saucepan from the heat and use a hand blender to blitz into a smooth, creamy soup.

4 Pour in the cream, season with salt and pepper and heat through without boiling.

5 Serve in warmed bowls, garnished with a drizzle of cream. Perfect served with warm, crusty bread.

SPICY FISH SOUP

with

ROASTED RED PEPPERS

Every region of Italy with a coastline has its own take on fish soup. This version is characteristic of the Campania region where I'm from originally. This recipe is so easy and being cooked in just one pot gives it extra appeal to busy people. You can use sustainably caught cod instead of haddock if you prefer, and please ensure the fish is extremely fresh. This soup can be served as a starter or a main meal; do make lots, as it will disappear really quickly.

Zuppa di pesce alla Torrese

serves 4

4 tablespoons olive oil
1 large red onion, peeled and finely chopped
1 teaspoon dried chilli flakes
200g roasted red peppers in brine from a jar, drained and sliced
150ml white wine
400ml hot fish stock
1 x 400g can chopped tomatoes
300g skinless haddock, cut into 5cm chunks
250g skinless red mullet, cut into 5cm chunks
16 large uncooked prawns, peeled
4 tablespoons freshly chopped flatleaf parsley
Salt, to taste

1   Heat the oil in a large saucepan over a medium heat and fry the onion, chilli and peppers for 2 minutes. Stir occasionally with a wooden spoon.

2   Pour in the wine and continue to cook for a further 2 minutes, allowing the alcohol to evaporate.

3   Pour in the fish stock, add the chopped tomatoes and season with salt. Bring to the boil, reduce the heat to low and simmer for 10 minutes, uncovered.

4   Add the fish and prawns, stir together and continue to cook for 4 minutes.

5   Stir in the parsley, check the seasoning and serve immediately with lots of crusty bread.

CARROTS AND ALMONDS

with

FRESH MINT AND CHILLI

There is almost nothing better than really fresh vegetables steamed or boiled al dente served with just a little salt and olive oil but, I must admit to occasionally getting a little bored of the same thing and have to create something with a bit of a twist – if it works, it gets to be in the next book, like this tasty carrot dish. Its flavours and textures are incredible together – try it as an accompaniment to any meat or fish.

Carote e mandorle alla menta

serves 4

6 large carrots
15 mint leaves, finely sliced
1 teaspoon dried chilli flakes
100g flaked almonds
8 tablespoons extra virgin olive oil
6 tablespoons white wine vinegar
Salt, to taste

Crispy salad leaves, to serve

1. Fill a medium saucepan with water and bring to the boil with 1 teaspoon of salt.

2. Peel the carrots and cut into 1cm rounds. Drop the carrots into the boiling water and cook for 3 minutes; drain well and place in a large bowl.

3. While the carrots are still hot, add the remaining ingredients to the bowl. Season with a little salt and gently mix together.

4. Set aside at room temperature for 10 minutes, allowing the flavours to combine beautifully. Gently stir every 2 minutes.

5. To serve, simply mix the marinated carrots into your favourite crispy salad.

SUPER-FAST OMELETTE

with

PARMA HAM

Breakfast, lunch or dinner – a tasty omelette is always a winner. This is one of the easiest, quickest recipes in the book yet it doesn't compromise on flavour. I love the combination of Parma ham and Parmesan cheese, which transports me back home to Italy, but there are numerous different variations that you can try such as cooked ham and Pecorino cheese or salami and Cheddar.

Frittatina al prosciutto

serves 1

2 large eggs
1 tablespoon freshly grated
Parmesan cheese
1 teaspoon salted butter
1 teaspoon olive oil
2 slices of Parma ham
Salt and white pepper, to taste

1 Break the eggs into a medium bowl and season with salt and pepper. Use a fork to gently whisk the eggs for 10 seconds. Add the Parmesan cheese and whisk for another 10 seconds.

2 Melt the butter with the oil in a 15cm frying pan over a medium heat. Tilt the pan so that the base and the sides are well greased. Increase the heat to its highest setting and, when the butter is foaming, pour in the eggs. Tilt the pan to spread the eggs evenly over the base. Leave it over the heat without moving and count to six.

3 Tilt the pan to 45 degrees and, using a tablespoon, draw the edges of the omelette into the centre. Tip the pan the other way and do the same thing.

4 Put the Parma ham slices in the middle of the omelette. Tilt the pan again and flip one side of the omelette into the centre then fold again.

5 Take the pan across to a warm serving plate and make the last fold when you tip the omelette onto the serving plate.

6 Serve immediately with warm crusty bread.

POACHED EGGS

with

CRISPY PANCETTA ON TOASTED CIABATTA

I made this for my best friend Marco years ago after a heavy night out – we still laugh about it today. I was explaining to him how I make crispy pancetta with soft poached eggs etc. He took a bite and said it was heaven but then proceeded to say that I could have just shut up while he had a sore head and served him his usual bacon and egg sandwich… OK, it is kind of a bacon and egg sandwich, but I am steadfast in my opinion that this is the ultimate Italian bacon and egg concoction and I'm not sure it can be compared to one from a greasy spoon: you tell me…

Uova e pancetta

serves 4

2 large round tomatoes
12 slices of pancetta
3 tablespoons white wine vinegar
8 large fresh eggs
8 slices of ciabatta bread,
1cm thick
4 teaspoons mayonnaise
Salt and black pepper, to taste

1   Preheat the grill to medium.

2   Cut the tomatoes into eight thick slices and spread out on a sheet of kitchen foil with the pancetta. Put on a baking tray and set aside.

3   Place 8 poaching rings in one or two frying pans (depending on their size) and pour in enough water to cover the base of the pan, at least 1cm deep. Pour in the vinegar and bring to the boil: reduce the heat so that the water starts to simmer. Gently break one egg into each ring and poach for 4 minutes until set.

4   Meanwhile, cook the tomatoes and pancetta under the grill for 2 minutes on each side.

5   Toast the ciabatta bread.

6   Place 2 slices of bread in the middle of each serving plate and spread the mayonnaise on the top side only. Arrange 2 slices of tomato on each slice of the ciabatta and top each one with 3 slices of pancetta.

7   Carefully place the poached eggs on top of the pancetta and sprinkle with a little salt and pepper. Serve immediately.

PIZZA-STYLE CIABATTA BREAD

with

OLIVES, MOZZARELLA AND ARTICHOKES

If you love pizza please try this recipe. It is quicker to make this from scratch than it is for you to pick up the phone, order a pizza and wait for it to be delivered. I know it will taste ten times better too! I have chosen olives, pesto and artichoke hearts as I think the combination is amazing – artichokes are still so underestimated but we Italians love them.

Pizzetta

serves 4

2 medium ciabattas, each about 130g, sliced in half horizontally
8 tablespoons passata
2 x 125g mozzarella balls, drained and thinly sliced
4 tablespoons green pesto
150g artichoke hearts in oil, drained and quartered
60g black pitted olives in brine or oil, drained and halved
12 cherry tomatoes, halved
Salt and black pepper, to taste

1 Preheat the oven to 200°C/gas 6.

2 Place the ciabatta slices on a baking tray, cut-side up.

3 Spread the passata evenly over each ciabatta half then top with the slices of mozzarella.

4 Spread the pesto over the mozzarella.

5 Scatter the remaining ingredients on top, season with salt and pepper and bake in the oven for 10 minutes.

6 Serve hot with a big glass of Italian cold white wine.

COUNTRY-STYLE BREAD

topped with

TOMATO AND GREEN OLIVES

Bruschetta has been around since at least the 15th century. It used to be simply a piece of bread grilled, rubbed with garlic and topped with extra virgin olive oil, salt and pepper, but nowadays the variations are numerous. One of the most popular versions outside Italy has to be tomato, basil, garlic and olive oil. However, on this occasion I've returned it to its homeland by adding in some olives – you won't be disappointed.

Bruschetta pomodoro e olive

serves 4

500g small plum tomatoes, quartered
10 basil leaves, shredded
5 tablespoons extra virgin olive oil, plus extra for brushing
150g pitted green olives in brine, drained and halved
1 loaf of country-style bread
2 garlic cloves, peeled
Salt and black pepper, to taste

1 Preheat a griddle pan over a medium heat.

2 Put the tomatoes in a large bowl. Add in three-quarters of the basil, the extra virgin olive oil and season with salt and pepper. Add the olives, mix together and cover with a tea towel. Set aside to marinate at room temperature for 5 minutes. Stir halfway through.

3 Meanwhile, cut 8 slices of bread from the loaf, each about 2cm thick. Brush a little oil on each side of the slices. Toast the bread on the griddle pan for 2 minutes on each side, until dark brown and crispy all over. Allow to cool slightly.

4 Lightly rub the garlic over both sides of the toasted bread. Top each slice with 2–3 tablespoons of the tomato mixture and arrange the bruschetta on a large serving plate.

5 Drizzle over any remaining juices from the bowl of tomatoes and sprinkle with the reserved basil.

6 Serve with a cold glass of beer as an appetiser, or as a starter.

STICKY SPICY LAMB SAUSAGES

These make a perfect little snack and are great as a simple starter. Lamb sausages make a change from the usual pork ones and, flavoured with rosemary, honey and chilli, they become irresistible little morsels: sticky and satisfying. You could remove the chilli if the kids are going to eat them; simply grind a little black pepper over the sausages instead.

Salsicciotti piccanti

serves 4

400g lamb chipolata sausages
2 tablespoons olive oil
1 tablespoon rosemary leaves,
finely chopped
1 teaspoon dried chilli flakes
2 tablespoons runny honey

1   Preheat the oven to 220°C/gas 7 and put a large ovenproof frying pan over a high heat.

2   Take each sausage and carefully twist in the middle so that you divide it into two. Cut through the twist so that you have two small cocktail sausages.

3   Pour the oil into the frying pan and add the sausages. Fry for 4 minutes, stirring occasionally with a wooden spoon.

4   Add the rosemary leaves to the frying pan with the chilli flakes. Continue to cook for 1 minute then stir in the honey.

5   Transfer the frying pan to the oven for 10 minutes.

6   Pile the little sausages in the middle of a chopping board and provide cocktail sticks for everyone. Make sure that you have plenty of cold drinks to serve with them.

BEEF CARPACCIO

with

ROCKET, BALSAMIC GLAZE AND PARMESAN

Carpaccio was created in Venice during the 20th century and has become the internationally recognised name for a dish of thinly sliced raw meat. It is said that in 1950 Countess Amalia Nani Mocenigo was advised by her doctor only to eat raw meat. Unfortunately, she didn't care for red meat, which she found tough and hard to digest. Giuseppe Cipriani, the owner of Harry's Bar in Venice, took up the challenge and created for her a dish of top-quality raw beef fillet, sliced very thinly and served with yellow mustard dressing. He named the recipe Carpaccio as the colours reminded him of the palette used by Venetian painter Vittore Carpaccio. My version uses balsamic glaze, its sweetness sharpened by the addition of capers, rather than the mustard used in the original.

Carpaccio di manzo con rucola e Parmigiano

serves 2

250g fillet of beef
4 tablespoons extra virgin olive oil
30g Parmesan shavings
2 tablespoons small capers in vinegar, drained
30g rocket leaves
3 tablespoons balsamic glaze
6 thin slices of ciabatta bread, toasted, to serve
Salt and black pepper, to taste

1   Cut the beef into very thin slices and place in a single layer between two sheets of clingfilm. Use a cooking hammer to beat the slices gently until they become very thin slivers.

2   Arrange the beef slivers in a single layer over the base of a cold large serving plate. Drizzle over the extra virgin olive oil and then sprinkle with a little salt and black pepper.

3   Scatter the Parmesan shavings and capers over the beef and pile the rocket leaves into the centre of the plate. Drizzle the balsamic glaze over the beef and rocket.

4   Serve with the toasted ciabatta.

CHICKEN

Il pollo

Chicken is probably the most popular meat and extremely versatile as you can cook it a number of ways in a variety of different dishes. Chicken breasts are great for quick meals as they are best when cooked for a short amount of time; if they are overcooked the meat tends to dry out. I've also included a few escalope recipes here as this technique of flattening the chicken breast makes the cooking time even faster.

CHICKEN AND CHORIZO SALAD

with

BEANS AND ROCKET LEAVES

Insalata di pollo e chorizo

Every now and then I go on a health kick and watch what I eat, especially in the evenings. However, there are only so many salads you can have before you start to get a bit bored, especially during the winter months – but this is an amazing option: filling, delicious and incredibly good for you but at the same time it won't leave you feeling hard done by, unlike some salads.

serves 4

100g can cannellini beans, drained and rinsed
100g can borlotti beans, drained and rinsed
20 cherry tomatoes, quartered
1 medium hot red chilli, deseeded and thinly sliced
1 garlic clove, peeled and finely sliced
2 tablespoons freshly squeezed lemon juice
8 tablespoons extra virgin olive oil
2 medium skinless, boneless chicken breasts, cut into 1cm strips
100g hot chorizo sausage, cut into thin round slices
60g rocket leaves
Salt, to taste

1   Put all the beans in a large bowl with the tomatoes, chilli and garlic. Pour over the lemon juice with half the olive oil, season with salt, toss all together and set aside.

2   Place a large frying pan over a high heat and pour in the remaining oil. Add the chicken strips and fry for 5 minutes, stirring occasionally with a wooden spoon.

3   Season with salt, add the chorizo and continue to fry for a further 2 minutes over a high heat.

4   Toss the rocket leaves through the bean salad and transfer to a large serving plate. Top with the crispy chicken and chorizo and serve immediately.

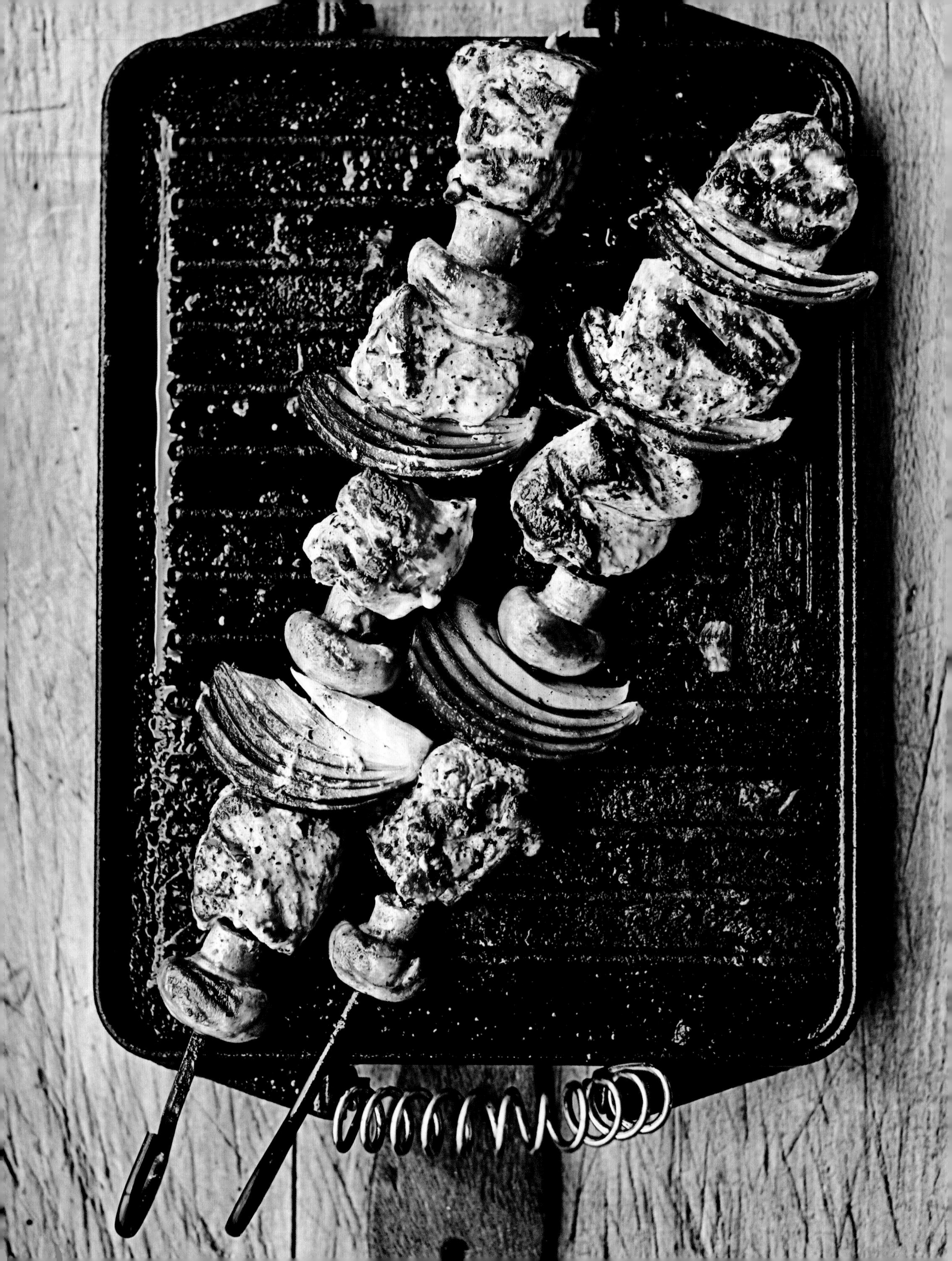

CHICKEN SKEWERS

marinated with

YOGURT AND MINT SAUCE

If it's pouring outside and you really fancy a barbecue-style dish, then these skewers are ideal. They are very light and extremely tasty, bringing a taste of summer into your life, whatever the season. Do add other vegetables like tomatoes or peppers to your skewers if you prefer.

Spiedini di pollo

serves 2

1 tablespoon ready-made mint sauce
1 tablespoon rosemary leaves, finely chopped
2 medium skinless, boneless chicken breasts, cut into 3cm chunks – ideally 8–10 big chunks
150g natural yogurt
1 large red onion, peeled and cut into 6 wedges
6 medium button mushrooms
Salt and black pepper, to taste
Crisps, to serve

1 Mix the yogurt, mint sauce and rosemary in a large bowl. Season with salt and pepper.

2 Add the chicken pieces and mix well to ensure that each piece is coated with the marinade. Leave to rest at room temperature for 8 minutes.

3 Preheat a griddle pan or a barbecue.

4 Thread the chicken onto two metal skewers (or wooden ones that have been soaked in water for at least 30 minutes), alternating each piece with onions and mushrooms.

5 Cook the skewers on the hot griddle pan or barbecue rack for 8 minutes, turning the meat to ensure that every side is coloured and cooked through.

6 Serve hot accompanied with a big bowl of your favourite crisps.

SKEWERED CHICKEN MEATBALLS
with
GARLIC YOGURT

This recipe came about one morning: the house was empty with the kids off playing football or rugby and I was in charge (as on most Sundays) of making lunch. I had every intention of making chicken meatballs in a tomato-based sauce but saw a glimpse of sun peeking through the clouds and ended up with meatball skewers instead, which was a lot quicker. They turned out to be really different and have now become a regular Sunday treat.

Polpettine di pollo

serves 4

300g minced chicken
1 large onion, finely chopped
½ teaspoon freshly ground black pepper
2 tablespoons freshly chopped mint
16 cherry tomatoes
3 tablespoons olive oil
Salt, to taste

For the garlic yogurt:
200ml natural yogurt
4 garlic cloves, peeled and crushed to a purée
1 teaspoon dried oregano
Salt, to taste

1 Preheat the grill to the highest setting.

2 Put the minced chicken in a large mixing bowl with the onion, black pepper and mint. Season with salt and mix together using your fingertips. Divide the mixture into four equal portions. Roll 5 balls from each portion to make 20 in total and set aside.

3 Thread one meatball on to a metal skewer, followed by a cherry tomato and continue until you have 5 meatballs and 4 cherry tomatoes on each skewer.

4 Transfer the skewers to a grill tray and brush with the olive oil. Cook under the grill for 10 minutes, turning the skewers regularly until browned all over.

5 Meanwhile, pour the yogurt into a bowl and add the garlic and oregano. Season with salt and mix together.

6 Put the skewered meatballs on a large serving plate and drizzle with the garlic yogurt. Serve hot with a cold beer or a glass of juice for the kids.

CHICKEN BURGERS

with

GARLIC AND THYME

I normally make this recipe with minced beef or pork but I was having friends round for lunch and their children didn't really like red meat so I made them burgers using chicken mince instead. It was such a success I decided to include it in this book. Minced chicken makes burgers that are much lighter in texture than ones made with red meat. I ended up swapping my beefburger for a chicken burger as it was so good.

Hamburger di pollo con aglio e timo

serves 4

500g minced chicken
2 teaspoons thyme leaves, finely chopped
60g fresh breadcrumbs
80g sun-dried tomatoes in oil, drained and finely sliced
1 garlic clove, peeled and finely chopped
50g freshly grated Parmesan cheese
1 egg, beaten
3 tablespoons olive oil, for greasing
4 good-quality burger baps
50g mixed salad leaves
4 tablespoons mayonnaise
Salt and black pepper, to taste

1 Use your hands to mix together the minced chicken, thyme, breadcrumbs, sun-dried tomatoes, garlic and Parmesan in a large bowl. Season with salt and pepper and pour in the beaten egg to bind the mixture. Continue to mix until well combined.

2 Preheat the oven to 150°C/gas 2 and put a griddle pan over a high heat.

3 Lightly grease the palms of your hands with olive oil and start to shape the chicken mixture into 4 large balls. Gently press each ball between your hands to create a burger patty.

4 Cook the burgers on the griddle pan for 4 minutes on each side.

5 Meanwhile, warm the baps in the oven.

6 Once the burgers are ready, cut the baps in half and put an equal layer of salad leaves on the bottom halves. Put a hot burger on top of the leaves, spread mayonnaise on the cut top half of the baps and close the burgers.

CHICKEN

in

LEMON AND PARSLEY SAUCE

This dish is actually my late grandfather's recipe. We lived near Sorrento, famous for the quality of its lemons, and he would always buy the biggest, freshest one he could find to make this recipe for us. During the hot steamy summers, this was one of our favourites as it is lovely, light and fresh on the palate. We would normally have this dish after loads of antipasti so we would have no room for more than the chicken and bread to dunk in the sauce but there's a range of serving possibilities – salad, veg or potatoes.

Pollo al limone e prezzemolo

serves 4

4 medium skinless, boneless chicken breasts
50g plain flour
4 tablespoons olive oil
80g butter
Juice of 2 lemons
50ml chicken stock
4 tablespoons freshly chopped flatleaf parsley
Salt and white pepper, to taste

1 Put the chicken breasts on a chopping board and use a sharp knife to cut each one horizontally into 2 thin slices.

2 Put the flour onto a large plate, season with salt and pepper and mix. Coat each side of the chicken breasts with the flour. Gently tap the chicken to discard any excess.

3 Heat the olive oil and half the butter in a large frying pan over a medium heat. Put the floured chicken in the pan and fry for 4 minutes on each side until it starts to brown and is cooked through. (Cook in batches if necessary.)

4 Transfer the cooked chicken slices to a large serving plate and cover with foil while you make the sauce.

5 Pour the lemon juice and the stock into the frying pan and use a wooden spoon to scrape all the brown bits from the edges and base into the sauce. Bring to the boil and stir for 1 minute. Add the chopped parsley and remaining butter and continue to stir for a further minute until it has a creamy texture.

6 To serve, place 2 slices of chicken in the middle of each serving plate and drizzle over the lemon and parsley sauce. Serve immediately with some crisp salad leaves or my warm New Potato Salad with Red Onions and Capers (see page 201).

CHICKEN BREAST

in

ROSEMARY AND ORANGE SAUCE

I'm not usually a big fan of meat with fruit but I do love this recipe. It's a simpler version of the French classic duck à l'orange but using chicken is a less fatty choice. I would normally recommend buying fruit and veg when they are in season but as this particular recipe calls for oranges, you can make it all year round. It's a classy way to serve chicken, with a subtle tangy flavour that everyone will enjoy.

Pollo in salsa di arance

serves 4

**6 tablespoons olive oil
4 medium boneless chicken
breasts, skin on
250g button mushrooms, cleaned
and quartered
3 tablespoons rosemary leaves
½ teaspoon dried chilli flakes
Juice of 2 large oranges
1 tablespoon red wine vinegar
Salt, to taste**

1 Heat the oil in a large frying pan over a medium heat and start to fry the chicken, skin-side down first, for 2 minutes on each side until browned. Remove the breasts from the pan and set aside.

2 Add the mushrooms and rosemary to the frying pan and fry for 4 minutes. Stir occasionally with a wooden spoon.

3 Sprinkle over the chilli and pour in the orange juice and the vinegar. Bring to the boil.

4 Return the chicken breasts to the pan and cook over a medium heat for 5 minutes to allow the chicken to finish cooking and the sauce to thicken. Turn the meat halfway through cooking and season with salt.

5 Serve immediately, placing the chicken breasts skin-side up surrounded by the orange sauce. Serve with a green salad.

CHICKEN BREAST

with

PINK PEPPERCORN AND GORGONZOLA SAUCE

Petto di pollo al Gorgonzola

If you are on a diet, you might want to turn to another page! The sauce I have created for this chicken is very rich and creamy but it's definitely a lovely indulgent treat. You can use a milder Dolcelatte rather than the Gorgonzola if you prefer, but don't try to make a low-calorie version of this by substituting anything lighter for the cream – you need the thickness of double cream to make the sauce work.

serves 4

50g salted butter
4 tablespoons olive oil
4 medium boneless chicken breasts, skin on
1 tablespoon pink peppercorns in brine, drained
100ml double cream
150g Gorgonzola cheese, cut into small cubes

1 Place a large non-stick frying pan over a medium heat, melt the butter with the oil and cook the chicken, skin-side down first, with the peppercorns for 4 minutes on each side until golden brown all over. Do not season with salt.

2 Transfer the chicken to a plate and cover with foil to keep warm while preparing the sauce. Leave the peppercorns in the frying pan.

3 Pour the cream into the pan and cook for 1 minute, stirring constantly with a wooden spoon.

4 Add the Gorgonzola and continue to stir constantly for 3 minutes allowing the cheese to melt and create a smooth sauce.

5 Place one chicken breast, skin-side up, in the middle of each serving plate and drizzle over the Gorgonzola and peppercorn sauce.

6 Serve immediately with vegetables of your choice and some warm crusty bread to mop up the sauce.

HUNTER-STYLE CHICKEN

in

A SPICY TOMATO SAUCE

Pollo piccante alla cacciatore

Chicken thighs are often underestimated but they are a fabulous cut of chicken, with more flavour than the white meat. Cooked in a one-pot stew they remain tender and juicy. This makes a warm and tasty supper; perfect for those colder evenings.

serves 4

5 tablespoons olive oil
150g diced pancetta
1 large white onion, peeled and finely sliced
2 tablespoons rosemary leaves, chopped
1 teaspoon dried chilli flakes
800g skinless boneless chicken thighs, each cut into 4 pieces
50ml red wine
2 x 400g cans of chopped tomatoes
2 bay leaves
Salt, to taste

1 Heat the oil in a heavy-based saucepan over a medium heat and fry the pancetta with the onion for 3 minutes. Stir occasionally with a wooden spoon.

2 Add the rosemary and chilli and continue to cook for a further minute.

3 Next add the chicken, season with salt and continue to cook for a further minute.

4 Pour in the wine and let it bubble before adding the chopped tomatoes and bay leaves. Cover with a lid and allow the chicken to gently simmer for 10 minutes. Stir occasionally.

5 Remove the lid and cook over a high heat for a further 3 minutes, allowing the sauce to thicken.

6 Serve with a large glass of Italian red wine and make sure there's plenty of warm crusty bread to soak up the sauce.

STICKY HONEY CHICKEN

with

SMOKED PAPRIKA

I absolutely love the flavours of this recipe – sweet, sticky and spicy. You can serve this with potatoes, rice, couscous or roasted vegetables but I find a simple crisp salad is enough to turn it into something a little bit special. You can use the marinade for pretty much any meat.

Pollo miele e paprika

serves 4

4 medium boneless chicken breasts, skin on
4 tablespoons runny honey
2 tablespoons tomato purée
2 teaspoons smoked paprika
Juice of 1 lime
1 tablespoon olive oil
Salt, to taste
Crusty bread, to serve

for the side salad:
150g rocket leaves
3 tablespoons extra virgin olive oil
4 tablespoons balsamic vinegar
50g Parmesan shavings
Salt, to taste

1 Preheat a griddle pan to very hot or light a barbecue if you prefer.

2 Put the chicken breasts on a chopping board between two sheets of clingfilm. Use a meat hammer or a rolling pin to flatten the chicken into escalopes 1cm thick.

3 Put the honey, tomato purée, smoked paprika and 2 pinches of salt in a large bowl. Pour in the lime juice and olive oil and mix together. Add the chicken and coat the breasts in the marinade evenly.

4 Cook the chicken on the griddle pan, skin-side down first, for 6 minutes on each side.

5 Meanwhile, prepare the salad by placing the rocket leaves in a large bowl. Pour over the oil and the balsamic vinegar and season with a couple of pinches of salt. Gently use your fingertips to toss together. Transfer the salad onto a large serving plate and scatter the shaved Parmesan on top.

6 Once the sticky chicken breasts are ready, serve together with a little crusty warm bread on the side.

CHICKEN BREASTS

with

CHERRY TOMATOES, MOZZARELLA AND BASIL

I'm from Naples, the city that invented pizza, and I've been brought up with them all my life. There is nothing quite like a freshly cooked Margherita pizza. I love the flavour so much that I have copied the ingredients and added them to this chicken recipe to give me that Italian kick I sometimes crave. It is important not to use buffalo mozzarella for this recipe as it is very milky and releases a lot of liquid when cooked.

Pollo Margherita

serves 4

4 skinless, boneless chicken breasts
6 tablespoons olive oil
4 garlic cloves, peeled and finely sliced
2 x 400g cans of cherry tomatoes
10 basil leaves, plus extra for garnish
3 x 125g mozzarella balls, drained and sliced (do not use buffalo mozzarella)
Salt and black pepper, to taste

1 Slash each chicken breast four times with a sharp knife, cutting as far as the middle of the breast.

2 Heat the olive oil in a large frying pan over a medium heat and gently fry the garlic and the chicken for 2 minutes on each side until golden all over.

3 Tip in the cherry tomatoes with the basil and season with salt and pepper. Stir all together.

4 Cook, uncovered, over a medium heat for 12 minutes. Halfway through cooking, turn over the chicken breasts.

5 Meanwhile, preheat the grill to the highest setting.

6 Remove the pan from the heat and place the mozzarella slices on top of the chicken breasts. Grind over some black pepper and put the pan under the grill for about 1 minute or until the cheese starts to melt. Protect the handle of the frying pan with foil if necessary.

7 To serve, pour some of the tomato sauce in the middle of each serving plate, place a breast of chicken on top and garnish with basil leaves. Serve with your favourite vegetables and warm crusty bread.

SPICED CHICKEN ESCALOPES

with

POTATO AND APPLE MASH

Scaloppine speziate con patate e mele

Chicken is extremely popular in our house and, for chicken fans like us, I wanted this chapter to include lots of options so that it's never bland or boring. The key to ensure your chicken dishes are appealing lies in the length of cooking (often the longer the cooking time, the drier the meat, especially the breast, becomes) and the kind of sauces you create. This one is especially light, more of a gravy than a heavy sauce, and, accompanied by my special mash, I hope my spicy escalopes will tick all your boxes.

serves 4

4 medium boneless chicken breasts, skin on
1½ tablespoons smoked paprika and ground coriander, mixed together
2 tablespoons salted butter
2 tablespoons olive oil

for the mash:
4 large potatoes, peeled and chopped into small pieces
1 tablespoon salted butter
2 cooking apples, peeled, cored and chopped into small pieces
1 tablespoon wholegrain mustard
Salt and white pepper, to taste

1   Put the potatoes in a medium saucepan and cover with boiling water from the kettle. Cook over a medium heat for 8–10 minutes until tender, drain and set aside.

2   Meanwhile, put the chicken breasts on a chopping board between two sheets of clingfilm. Use a meat hammer or a rolling pin to flatten the chicken into escalopes 1cm thick. Rub the spice mix all over both sides of the chicken breasts.

3   Melt the butter with the oil in a large non-stick frying pan over a medium heat and cook the chicken for 5 minutes on each side, skin-side down first. Remove from the pan and transfer to a warm plate, cover with foil and set aside.

4   Add 4 tablespoons of hot water to the frying pan and use a wooden spoon to move the juices around and loosen any meaty bits from the pan to make a quick gravy.

5   For the mash, melt the butter in the same saucepan used to cook the potatoes, add the apples and cook over a high heat for 3 minutes. Stir occasionally with a wooden spoon. Tip the drained potatoes into the saucepan, season with salt and pepper, add the mustard and roughly mash together.

6   Put each chicken breast on a large serving plate, surround with the mash and drizzle over the quick gravy.

CHICKEN SALTIMBOCCA

with

PARMA HAM AND MARSALA

I came up with this recipe because some friends of mine told me they were watching their weight but they loved my Pollo al Marsala dish and wished they could have a similar recipe but without the cream. Well, I got to work and here is the result (let's not tell them about the butter!). It still wows with that Marsala flavour but lets other ingredients such as the Parma ham zap your tastebuds. A really lovely recipe that can be served with anything.

Saltimbocca

serves 4

4 medium skinless, boneless chicken breasts
4 slices of Parma ham, cut in half widthways
8 large sage leaves
6 tablespoons olive oil
50g salted butter
200ml Marsala wine
Salt and black pepper, to taste

1 Put the chicken breasts on a chopping board between two sheets of clingfilm. Use a meat hammer or a rolling pin to flatten the chicken into escalopes 1cm thick.

2 Cut the escalopes in half widthways to give 8 pieces in total. Season with a little salt and pepper and lay a piece of Parma ham on each piece. Top with one sage leaf and secure with a cocktail stick.

3 Heat the oil and half the butter in a large frying pan over a medium heat. Place the saltimbocca in the pan, ham-side down. Cook for 2 minutes until browned. Turn and cook for a further 3 minutes until just cooked through. Transfer to a plate and cover with foil to keep warm.

4 Pour the Marsala wine into the hot frying pan and use a match or a lighter to flame the alcohol.

5 Once the flames die down, use a wooden spoon to deglaze the pan by scraping up the meaty bits from the bottom. Simmer over a high heat for 1 minute until slightly reduced. Stir in the remaining butter and check the seasoning.

6 Return the chicken and any juices to the pan, turning them in the sauce for 30 seconds. Remove the pan from the heat and remove the cocktail sticks from the saltimbocca.

7 Put 2 pieces of saltimbocca on each serving plate and drizzle with the Marsala sauce. Enjoy with a glass of cold medium white wine.

CHICKEN IN A MARTINI

and

SAGE SAUCE

I really like cooking with alcohol as it enhances flavours. You often find recipes with wine in the ingredients but I wanted to try something a bit different. There is always a bottle of Martini Bianco in our fridge, hence a recipe had to come about with it as the star. I think you will love this recipe and be pleasantly surprised how the sweetness of the Martini with the salt, pepper and sage create a lovely flavour.

Scaloppine al Martini e salvia

serves 4

4 medium skinless, boneless chicken breasts
6 tablespoons plain flour
100g salted butter, plus
1 tablespoon extra for the sauce
2 tablespoons olive oil
4 large sage leaves, finely sliced
200ml sweet Martini Bianco
Salt and white pepper, to taste

1 Put the chicken breasts on a chopping board between two sheets of clingfilm. Use a meat hammer or a rolling pin to flatten the chicken into escalopes 0.5cm thick.

2 Spread the flour on a flat plate and season with salt and pepper.

3 Put a large frying pan over a medium heat and start to melt the butter with the olive oil and sage.

4 Lay the chicken breasts in the seasoned flour and coat on both sides. Gently tap the chicken to discard any excess.

5 Put the chicken in the frying pan and fry for 3 minutes on one side. Turn over the meat and cook for a further minute. Pour in the Martini and use a match or a lighter to flame the alcohol. Cook for a further 2 minutes and season with salt and pepper.

6 Transfer the escalopes to a large serving plate.

7 Add the extra tablespoon of butter to the Martini sauce. Mix well over medium heat and immediately pour over the chicken breasts.

8 Serve with a simple green salad dressed with extra virgin olive oil, a squeeze of fresh lemon juice and a pinch of salt.

CHICKEN
in
A VIN SANTO SAUCE

This is my wife's favourite meal. I made it for her years ago when we first met and she was hooked. If I ever want to get in her good books or have her full attention (you know what I mean) – this is the meal I prepare. It's a lovely creamy dish and yet doesn't leave you feeling too full. I often serve this with peas and pancetta or crushed potatoes but rice, bread and couscous are also lovely side dishes.

Pollo al Vin Santo

serves 2

2 medium skinless, boneless chicken breasts
2 tablespoons plain flour, for dusting
3 tablespoons olive oil
6 tablespoons Vin Santo
150ml double cream
Salt and white pepper, to taste

1   Put the chicken breasts on a chopping board between two sheets of clingfilm. Use a meat hammer or a rolling pin to flatten the chicken into escalopes 0.5cm thick.

2   Lightly coat each chicken breast with flour. Gently tap the chicken to discard any excess.

3   Put a large frying pan over a medium heat, add the olive oil and fry the chicken breasts for 3 minutes on one side. Turn the meat over and cook for a further minute.

4   Pour in the Vin Santo and use a match or a lighter to flame the alcohol.

5   Once the flames die down, reduce the heat, pour in the cream, season with salt and pepper and cook, uncovered, for 5 minutes allowing the sauce to thicken. Stir occasionally.

6   Put a chicken breast on each serving plate and drizzle over the delicious Vin Santo sauce.

7   Serve immediately with a couscous salad (see page 194).

STUFFED CHICKEN BREAST

with

ONION MARMALADE AND GOAT'S CHEESE

I often make a goat's cheese and caramelised onion puff pastry parcel as a starter and everyone raves about it so I thought I'd incorporate those flavours into a chicken dish to serve as a main meal. Chicken can be bland and yet with a few ingredients added, it transforms into something really special. If you want a milder flavour than the goat's cheese use mozzarella – I've even used cream cheese, which also works well.

Petto di pollo ripieno

serves 4

4 medium boneless, skinless chicken breasts
4 tablespoons red onion marmalade
100g goat's cheese
4 tablespoons olive oil
12 thyme sprigs

for the side salad:
110g bag of mixed salad leaves
3 tablespoons extra virgin olive oil
2 tablespoons balsamic vinegar
Salt and black pepper, to taste

1 Preheat the oven to 200°C/gas 6.

2 Place the chicken breasts on a chopping board and use a sharp knife to slice in half horizontally, making sure that you don't cut all the way through. Open out each chicken breast like a book.

3 Spread the onion marmalade evenly over the opened-out chicken breasts then crumble over the goat's cheese. Fold each breast in half and secure with a cocktail stick.

4 Place the stuffed breasts on a baking tray and brush all over with olive oil. Sprinkle the tops with salt and pepper and scatter over the thyme sprigs. Roast in the oven for 13 minutes.

5 One minute before the chicken is ready, place the salad leaves in a large bowl and toss in the extra virgin olive oil and balsamic vinegar. Season with a little salt and pepper.

6 Remove the cocktail sticks from the chicken breasts and serve immediately with the salad and warm bread on the side.

CHICKEN AND ASPARAGUS STIR-FRY

with

BALSAMIC GLAZE

I love a good stir-fry and most of the time I just make one with anything and everything I've got in the fridge. However, sometimes I like to give one ingredient the spotlight and in this recipe I've chosen asparagus. Did you know that asparagus is 93 per cent water? It is extremely low in calories and very low in sodium as well as an amazing source of calcium, magnesium, vitamin B, zinc, protein, beta-carotene, vitamin C, vitamin E, vitamin K, thiamin, riboflavin, rutin, niacin, folic acid, iron, phosphorus, potassium, copper, manganese and selenium. I'm not even sure what all these do but what an amazing vegetable!

Pollo e asparagi in padella

serves 4

200g long grain white rice
3 medium boneless and skinless chicken breasts, sliced into 5cm lengths
2 tablespoons runny honey
3 tablespoons balsamic vinegar
1 tablespoon sesame seed oil
4 tablespoons olive oil
100g chestnut mushrooms, cleaned and quartered
300g asparagus spears, cut into 5cm lengths
1 tablespoon sesame seeds
Salt and black pepper, to taste

1 Put the rice in a medium saucepan, cover with boiling water from the kettle, add a teaspoon of salt and cook until tender. Stir occasionally.

2 Meanwhile, put the sliced chicken breasts into a large bowl. Pour in the honey, balsamic vinegar and sesame seed oil. Mix well and leave to marinate for 3 minutes.

3 Heat a wok over a high heat and pour in the olive oil. Fry the mushrooms and asparagus for 2 minutes, stirring constantly with a wooden spoon.

4 Reduce the heat to medium, add the chicken and all the marinade to the wok and continue to cook for a further 10 minutes. Stir occasionally. (If the sauce gets too thick, pour in a little hot water from the kettle.)

5 Check for seasoning and sprinkle over the sesame seeds.

6 Serve immediately in the middle of a large serving plate surrounded by the cooked rice.

CRISPY CHICKEN IN BREADCRUMBS

with

TOMATO SALSA

These days many people buy ready-made chicken escalopes but I promise you, homemade ones are far superior in terms of taste and the satisfaction that comes from knowing that what you are eating is all chicken rather than 10 per cent chicken and the rest almost all bread. And I guarantee that the combination of this really crispy coating (which you wouldn't get by baking ready-made escalopes) with the fresh salsa dressing will be so worth the three extra plates you need to wash up – plus the meal will cost you less than buying escalopes from a supermarket.

Pollo alla Milanese

serves 2

8 tablespoons olive oil
2 medium skinless, boneless chicken breasts
Plain flour, for dusting
2 eggs, beaten in a bowl
70g toasted fine breadcrumbs

for the salsa:
15 yellow cherry tomatoes, quartered
80g pitted green olives
5 fresh mint leaves, sliced
3 tablespoons extra virgin olive oil

for the spinach:
2 tablespoons olive oil
250g spinach leaves
1 garlic clove, peeled and finely sliced
2 pinches of dried chilli flakes
Salt and black pepper, to taste

1   For the salsa, put the tomatoes, olives and mint leaves in a large bowl, drizzle over the extra virgin olive oil and season with salt and pepper. Mix well and set aside.

2   Put the chicken breasts on a chopping board between two sheets of clingfilm. Use a meat hammer or a rolling pin to flatten the chicken into escalopes 0.5cm thick.

3   Have ready the flour and beaten eggs and put the breadcrumbs on a large plate. Lightly dust the breasts with flour, dip in the beaten eggs and finally coat in the breadcrumbs.

4   Heat the olive oil in a large frying pan over a medium heat and gently fry the chicken for 4 minutes on each side until golden and crispy all over.

5   Meanwhile, cook the spinach. Heat the olive oil in a large frying pan over a medium heat and fry the spinach with the garlic and chilli. Season with salt and cook for about 3 minutes until wilted, stirring continuously with a wooden spoon. Remove from the heat and set aside.

6   Transfer the chicken escalopes to kitchen paper to drain any excess oil. Season with salt and pepper.

7   To serve, place each escalope in the centre of 2 serving plates, scatter the tomato salsa on top and serve immediately with the spicy spinach.

MEAT

La carne

This chapter includes recipes using pork, lamb and beef and a variety of cuts of meat. Steaks, cutlets and chops are all brilliant for fast meals but I've also included recipes using minced meat for my Italian twist on popular dishes such as burgers and cottage pie. From simple salads to hearty suppers– I've even managed to include a quick-cook pie and stew – there's a dish to satisfy every appetite and occasion.

POTTED EGGS

and

HAM

I often have this as a simple supper but it also makes a great Sunday morning brunch with the family. It's a perfect quick dish as you're cooking complete meals in individual portions so there is no serving up at the table, and little washing up afterwards. Eggs, spinach and ham is a classic Florentine combination.

Ciotoline di uova e spinaci

serves 4

3 tablespoons olive oil
800g baby spinach leaves
Pinch of ground nutmeg
8 slices of Italian cooked ham with herbs
150ml double cream
Small bunch of chives, chopped
50g freshly grated Parmesan cheese
8 eggs
8 thick slices of sourdough
Butter, to serve
Salt and black pepper, to taste

1 Preheat the oven to 190°C/gas 5 and put a large wok over a high heat.

2 Add the oil and spinach to the hot wok and allow to wilt for 5 minutes. Stir occasionally. Once it has wilted and all the water has evaporated, season with salt, black pepper and a pinch of nutmeg.

3 Line 4 individual serving dishes about 15cm in diameter (or simply use large ramekins) with 2 slices of the ham. Divide the spinach between the dishes and spread it out over the bottom.

4 Pour the cream into a large bowl and add the chopped chives and Parmesan cheese. Season with black pepper and mix.

5 Crack two eggs into each ham-lined dish and pour in the cream mixture, ensuring the chives are distributed evenly. Transfer the dishes to a baking tray and cook in the oven for 10 minutes.

6 Meanwhile, toast the sourdough.

7 Serve the potted eggs with hot buttered toast.

MARSALA PEAR SALAD

with

PARMA HAM CRISPS AND GORGONZOLA CHEESE

This is a brilliant-tasting and simple starter, one that we often serve at Christmas before the main event. It is not one you can make and plate up in advance as the warm pears quickly wilt the salad leaves. However, as you can have it prepared and cooked in 15 minutes, it's perfect for when you have a huge roast to contend with. Pears can sometimes be hard but served warm and sticky they are divine with salty Parma ham and creamy rich cheese.

Insalata di pere e prosciutto crudo

serves 4

12 slices of Parma ham
2 pears (not too ripe)
2 tablespoons salted butter
4 tablespoons runny honey
2 tablespoons fresh rosemary leaves
3 tablespoons Marsala wine
110g bag of crisp salad leaves
2 tablespoons extra virgin olive oil
Juice of ½ lemon
150g Gorgonzola cheese
Salt and black pepper, to taste

1   Preheat the oven to 180°C/gas 4.

2   Spread out the slices of Parma ham on two baking trays and cook in the oven for 8 minutes. Remove from the oven and set aside to cool and harden.

3   Quarter the pears, remove the core and cut each quarter in half.

4   Melt the butter in a medium frying pan and add the pears. Drizzle with honey and add the rosemary. Cook for 1 minute until the juices are thick and sticky.

5   Pour in the Marsala wine and continue to cook for a further 2 minutes. Stir occasionally then remove from the heat and set aside.

6   Put the salad leaves in a large bowl and dress with the olive oil and lemon juice. Season with salt and pepper and divide between 4 serving plates.

7   Break the Gorgonzola into small pieces and add them to the dressed salad leaves.

8   Top with the warm pear slices and crumble over the Parma ham crisps. Drizzle over the honey and rosemary sauce and serve immediately.

LOADED PORK TOASTIES

For me, one of the simplest pleasures in life is a mortadella sandwich. Whenever I am in Italy, a quick stop-off at the local deli and I am in heaven – thin slices of mortadella piled high in a fresh ciabatta roll. Here I've used the idea to make a tortilla toastie that's loaded with Italian hams.

Tostini di mozzarella e salumi

serves 4

4 large tortilla wraps
200g grated mozzarella cheese
12 slices salami Napoli
100g sliced mortadella
4 slices of prosciutto cotto
(cooked ham)
Salt, to taste

for the quick tomato salsa:
2 tablespoons olive oil
1 small red onion, finely sliced
250g baby plum tomatoes, halved
1 tablespoon caster sugar
1 tablespoon balsamic vinegar
Pinch of dried chilli flakes
10 basil leaves

1   First make the tomato salsa. Heat the olive oil in a medium frying pan and cook the onion for 2 minutes. Stir occasionally with a wooden spoon. Add the tomatoes, sugar, balsamic vinegar and chilli flakes. Stir everything together until the tomatoes start to burst, remove from the heat and season with salt. Stir in the basil leaves and set aside.

2   Place 2 tortillas on a chopping board and sprinkle with half the grated mozzarella. Top with the salami, mortadella and ham. Scatter over the remaining mozzarella and put the remaining 2 tortillas on top. Press down lightly.

3   Gently transfer one of the tortilla sandwiches to a large frying pan over a medium heat and cook for 1 minute or until golden and crispy. Use a fish slice to turn it over and cook the other side for a further 30 seconds. Reduce the heat if the tortilla is turning too brown before the cheese is oozing and melted.

4   Remove the tortilla sandwich from the frying pan and repeat the process with the other sandwich.

5   Cut the crispy tortillas into triangles and serve with the quick tomato salsa.

CREAMY SAUSAGE

and

BROCCOLI RAGÙ

Sausages can take a while to cook, so when you are short of time this is a great dish to make. Using sausages instead of pork mince speeds things up as they are already packed full of flavour and perfectly seasoned. If you are no fan of broccoli, you could always use peas, asparagus or some sugar snap peas.

Ragù di salsicce e broccoletti

serves 4

200g long grain rice
4 tablespoons olive oil
4 spring onions, roughly chopped
A few sprigs of thyme
6 good-quality Italian pork sausages
200g tenderstem broccoli
50ml white wine
1 tablespoon vegetable stock powder
100ml crème fraîche
30g Parmesan cheese
Salt and white pepper, to taste

1   Measure the rice into a cup and then tip into a large saucepan with a tight-fitting lid. Pour in 1½ times the amount of boiling water from the kettle and add a good pinch of salt. Put a lid on and bring to a simmer. Gently cook for 10 minutes then turn the heat off and leave to stand.

2   Heat the olive oil in a large frying pan and fry the spring onions and thyme leaves for 2 minutes. Stir occasionally with a wooden spoon.

3   Meanwhile, remove the sausagemeat from the skins and break the meat up using your fingertips. Add to the frying pan and cook for a further 5 minutes. Stir occasionally.

4   While the meat is browning, chop the broccoli into 1cm pieces. Add to the frying pan and cook for 3 minutes.

5   Pour in the white wine, stir all together and continue to cook for a further 2 minutes. Stir in the stock powder and crème fraîche. Season with salt and pepper.

6   Serve the ragù over the rice and sprinkle the top with freshly grated Parmesan.

PORK CHOPS

with

SAGE AND CANNELLINI BEANS

Maiale burro e salvia

Italians love to cook with canned beans and will always have a good stock of them in their cupboards. They are so versatile and there is no need for long soaking and cooking; it's all done for you. Buy good-quality ones and give them a thorough rinse under cold water to remove the water that they have been canned in for freshness and flavour. White cannellini beans are an Italian staple: their mealy texture and slightly nutty flavour is great with pork.

serves 4

4 tablespoons olive oil
4 x 200–250g pork loin chops
4 sprigs of thyme
2 garlic cloves, peeled
2 x 400g cans of cannellini beans, drained
50ml white wine
1 teaspoon vegetable stock powder
100ml water
100ml double cream
50g unsalted butter
16 small sage leaves
Salt and white pepper, to taste

1   Heat half the olive oil in a large frying pan and cook the chops with the thyme for 4 minutes on each side.

2   Meanwhile, pour the remaining oil into a medium frying pan. Grate in the garlic and add the beans. Stir and cook for 2 minutes. Pour the wine over the beans and cook for a further 2 minutes. Stir occasionally.

3   Sprinkle the stock powder over the beans, pour in the water and gently cook for 1 minute. Pour in the cream and continue to simmer for 3 minutes.

4   Meanwhile, transfer the pork chops to a plate. Season with salt and pepper, cover with foil and set aside.

5   Melt the butter in the pan used to cook the chops. Add 12 of the sage leaves and fry for 1 minute until crisp. Set aside.

6   Shred the remaining sage leaves and stir into the beans. Season well with salt and pepper and divide the beans between 4 serving plates.

7   Place the pork chops on top of the beans and drizzle over the sage butter. Top with the crispy sage leaves.

PORK TENDERLOIN

with

LEMON AND THYME

Tenderloin is a lean cut of pork and if it is overcooked it can become really dry. Browning it quickly and then cooking it in a sauce is a perfect way to keep it moist. If you are ever roasting it, just keep a really close eye on it or simply wrap it in bacon to help keep the moisture in.

Medaglioni di maiale al limone

serves 4

3 tablespoons plain flour
600g pork tenderloin, cut into 8 thick slices
3 tablespoons olive oil
2 unwaxed lemons, cut into 8 slices
A few sprigs of thyme
150ml white wine
100ml hot chicken stock
Salt and black pepper, to taste

1 Put the flour on a plate and season with salt and pepper.

2 Lightly dip the pork slices into the flour then shake off the excess so that they are lightly coated.

3 Heat the olive oil in a large frying pan and cook the pork slices for 1 minute on each side.

4 Transfer the pork to a plate, cover with foil and set aside.

5 Add the lemon slices to the pan along with the thyme leaves and cook for 2 minutes. Stir occasionally with a wooden spoon. Pour in the white wine and bring to a simmer. Cook for a further 2 minutes.

6 Pour in the stock, bring to the boil and return the pork to the sauce. Cook for a further 3 minutes until the sauce has slightly thickened and the pork is cooked through. Season with salt and pepper.

7 Serve the pork on a large serving plate and drizzle over the delicious lemon and thyme sauce. Accompany with the New Potato Salad with Red Onions and Capers (see page 201) if you wish.

CRISPY BREADED PORK

with

APPLE SAUCE AND WATERCRESS SALAD

Milanese di maiale con salsa di mele

It seems as if there is a universal law that if something is coated in breadcrumbs it will taste amazing, and this dish is no exception. Just remember to get your pan nice and hot so that the coating is extra crispy without the meat being overcooked. You don't need to serve anything other than a little sweet apple sauce and some peppery salad with these tasty pork steaks.

serves 2

2 x 200g boneless pork loin steaks
2 tablespoons plain flour
Pinch of smoked paprika
1 egg
100g dried fine breadcrumbs
3 tablespoons olive oil
Salt and freshly ground black pepper, to taste

for the sauce:
2 large cooking apples, peeled, quartered, cored and cut into 2cm cubes
30g salted butter
2 tablespoons water
2 tablespoons caster sugar

for the salad:
1 teaspoon honey
1 tablespoon wholegrain mustard
Juice of ½ lemon
4 tablespoons extra virgin olive oil
100g watercress
25g walnut halves

1 Put the apples for the sauce in a small saucepan with the butter, water and caster sugar. Cover with a lid and cook over a low heat for 8 minutes. Stir occasionally with a wooden spoon.

2 Meanwhile, place the pork steaks between two pieces of clingfilm and use a meat hammer or rolling pin to bash them until they are 0.5cm thick.

3 Put the flour in a shallow bowl, season with salt and pepper and a pinch of paprika. Beat the egg in a second shallow bowl. Tip the breadcrumbs into a third bowl. Dip each piece of pork first into the flour, then into the egg and finally into the breadcrumbs.

4 Heat the olive oil in a medium frying pan and cook the coated pork for 4 minutes on each side.

5 Meanwhile, make the salad dressing. Put the honey, mustard, lemon juice and extra virgin olive oil in a jam jar and season with salt and pepper. Screw on the lid and shake everything together.

6 Transfer the pork to a plate covered with kitchen paper to drain off any excess oil.

7 Put the watercress in a serving bowl with the walnuts and coat with the salad dressing.

8 Serve the breaded pork with the watercress salad and apple sauce.

PORK CHOPS AND PANCETTA

with

COURGETTE FRITTERS

These courgette fritters are a great way to get the kids to eat veg. They look like potato rösti but are much quicker to cook and once topped with pancetta and soured cream the sweet courgettes will fool even the fussiest of eaters. You can use the fritters as a side dish for any main course.

Maiale e frittatine di zucchine

serves 4

3 tablespoons olive oil
4 x 130–150g pork chops
12 slices pancetta
2 tablespoons runny honey
150ml soured cream
Cayenne pepper, to dust
Salt and black pepper, to taste

for the courgette fritters:
3 tablespoons olive oil
4 courgettes
5 tablespoons self-raising flour
50g finely grated Parmesan cheese
1 egg yolk

1 Preheat the oven to 200°C/gas 6 and put two large frying pans over a high heat. One must have a heatproof handle.

2 Heat the olive oil in the frying pan with the heatproof handle and fry the pork chops for 3 minutes on each side. Remove from the pan and set aside to rest.

3 Meanwhile, coarsely grate the courgettes into a large bowl. Stir in the flour and the Parmesan. Add the egg yolk and season well with black pepper and a little salt. Mix everything together and shape into 8 fritters.

4 Add the remaining olive oil to the preheated frying pan and fry the courgette fritters for 3 minutes on each side.

5 While the fritters are cooking on the first side, fry the pancetta for 2 minutes in the pan used for the pork. Add the chops back to the pan and drizzle over the honey. Warm through for 1 minute.

6 Meanwhile, season the soured cream with some salt and black pepper.

7 Serve the fritters with the pork chops, crispy pancetta and a good dollop of soured cream.

8 Drizzle over the sticky honey sauce from the pan and dust the top with a little cayenne pepper.

PORK MEDALLIONS

in

MARSALA AND MUSHROOM SAUCE

Tenderloin is an expensive cut of meat, so adding meaty mushrooms means that you can stretch it a little further. 'Medallion', incidentally, is simply a cook's term for the thick rounds cut from the tenderloin. Marsala, a product of Sicily, is, like port, a fortified wine, which Italians love to drink and cook with. If you don't have any Marsala in the cupboard, try using sherry or a little white wine. When wild mushrooms are in season, use those if you can get your hands on any – the flavour will be much better.

Medaglioni di maiale

serves 4

2 tablespoons olive oil
500g pork tenderloin, cut into
8 thick slices
200g chestnut mushrooms,
halved
100ml Marsala wine
100ml hot chicken stock
150ml double cream
3 tablespoons chopped tarragon
leaves
40g salted butter
Salt and black pepper, to taste

for the potatoes:
500g baby new potatoes
Zest of 1 unwaxed lemon
Small bunch of chives, finely
chopped

1 Put the potatoes in a large saucepan, cover with boiling water from the kettle, add 2 teaspoons of salt and cook for 10 minutes.

2 Heat the oil in a large frying pan and cook the medallions of pork for 2 minutes on each side. Transfer to a plate, cover with foil and set aside.

3 Add the mushrooms to the frying pan and cook for 2 minutes. Stir occasionally with a wooden spoon.

4 Put the pork back into the frying pan with the mushrooms and pour in the Marsala. Allow to bubble for 2 minutes then add the stock and cream. Stir in the tarragon and cook for 5 minutes. Season with salt and pepper.

5 Drain the potatoes and return to the same saucepan, stir in the butter, lemon zest and chopped chives. Season with salt and pepper.

6 Put 2 pork medallions in the centre of 4 serving plates, pour over the Marsala and mushroom sauce and serve immediately with the potatoes.

GAMMON STEAKS

with

HONEY AND MUSTARD APPLES

Gammon is a great cut of pork and it is also fairly cheap to buy. Its strong salty flavour means it goes perfectly with something sweet. In this case I have chosen apples – a classic combination of ingredients that you will find in most European cuisines.

Bistecca di maiale con miele e mostarda

serves 2

2 gammon steaks
2 tablespoons olive oil
2 tablespoons runny honey
2 teaspoons Dijon mustard
1 tablespoon wholegrain mustard
1 eating apple
25g butter
1 tablespoon cider vinegar
Black pepper, to taste

1 Put a large frying pan over a high heat.

2 Snip the rind off the gammon steaks to prevent them from curling up as they cook.

3 Add the oil to the hot frying pan and cook the steaks for 3 minutes on one side until golden brown.

4 Meanwhile, combine the honey and mustards in a small bowl.

5 Turn the steaks over and continue to cook for a further 3 minutes.

6 Transfer the gammon to a plate and cover with foil to keep warm. Set aside.

7 Quarter the apple, remove the core and cut each quarter in half giving you 8 wedges.

8 Add the butter and apples to the frying pan and cook for 2 minutes. Pour in the cider vinegar and continue to cook for 1 minute, stirring with a wooden spoon.

9 Add the honey and mustard mixture and allow to bubble for a further minute. Stir together. Season with black pepper.

10 Serve the gammon with the warm sticky apples and some of the sauce poured over.

GAMMON STEAKS

with

FRUITY BULGAR WHEAT

I often make this tasty dish because I usually have raisins, dried apricots or cranberries in the cupboard along with a lone apple or pear in the fruit bowl. Bulgar wheat is readily available in supermarkets but you could also use couscous. Either way, gammon steak is an ideal meat to serve with it as the fruit and honey used here nicely balance its saltiness. So go easy on the salt when seasoning the bulgar wheat but you can load up on the black pepper.

Bistecche di maiale con miele e rosmarino

serves 2

100g bulgar wheat
1 teaspoon chicken or vegetable stock powder
3 tablespoons olive oil
2 gammon steaks
2 tablespoons fresh rosemary leaves
1 pear
2 stalks of celery
3 tablespoons honey
2 tablespoons extra virgin olive oil
Juice of 1 lemon
50g raisins (or chopped dried apricots or cranberries)
2 tablespoons chopped flatleaf parsley
Salt and black pepper, to taste

1   Tip the bulgar wheat into a bowl, sprinkle over the stock powder and pour over 150ml boiling water from the kettle. Stir, then cover the bowl with clingfilm. Set aside for 15 minutes.

2   Heat the olive oil in a medium frying pan and cook the gammon steaks with the rosemary for 5 minutes on each side.

3   Meanwhile, finely dice the pear (no need to peel; just cut around the core) and celery.

4   Transfer the gammon to a plate, cover with foil and set aside to keep warm.

5   Add the honey to the frying pan and pour in 2 tablespoons of water. Season with black pepper and stir together to create a sauce.

6   Use a fork to break up the cooked bulgar wheat and separate all the grains. Drizzle the extra virgin olive oil over the bulgar wheat with the juice of 1 lemon. Stir in the pear, celery, raisins and flatleaf parsley. Season with a little salt and plenty of black pepper.

7   Serve the gammon with the bulgar wheat and drizzle over the honey sauce.

ITALIAN SAUSAGE STEW

with

PEPPERS AND CRUNCHY CROUTONS

There is nothing more comforting than a big bowl of stew. My favourite way to eat it is with crunchy croutons that ~~cook up all the juices and soften slightly – fantastico!~~

Stufato di salsicce e peperoni

serves 4

1 ciabatta, cut into 2cm cubes
6 tablespoons olive oil
4 sprigs of thyme
1 red pepper
1 yellow pepper
2 garlic cloves, peeled and sliced
2 rosemary stalks
10 Italian pork sausages
2 x 400g cans cherry tomatoes
100g pitted black olives in brine or oil, drained
5 tablespoons freshly chopped flatleaf parsley
Salt and black pepper, to taste

1   Preheat the oven to 180°C/gas 4.

2   Put the ciabatta cubes on a baking tray. Drizzle over 2 tablespoons of olive oil, season with salt and pepper and sprinkle over thyme leaves. Toss everything together and transfer to the oven for 15 minutes until crispy.

3   Meanwhile, cut the peppers in half, discard the green stem, membrane and seeds, and roughly slice.

4   Put a medium saucepan over a high heat. Pour the remaining oil into the pan, add the garlic, peppers and rosemary and fry for 3 minutes. Stir occasionally with a wooden spoon.

5   While the peppers cook, remove the sausagemeat from the skins and make 3 small meatballs per sausage. Set aside.

6   Pour the tomatoes into the saucepan with the peppers and bring to the boil. Add the sausage meatballs to the sauce, gently stir and cook for 13 minutes, uncovered. Stir occasionally.

7   Don't forget to check the croutons!

8   Once the meatballs are cooked, season with salt and pepper. Finally, stir the olives and parsley into the stew and serve immediately with the delicious croutons.

SPICY CHORIZO

and

BORLOTTI BEAN STEW WITH POLENTA

I know chorizo is Spanish but it is so good I have stolen some for this recipe! There are two different types: 'eating' chorizo, which is like a salami that can be eaten raw, and 'cooking' chorizo which is like any other sausage but it's full of spices and paprika.

Stufato piccante con polenta

serves 4

8 'cooking' chorizo sausages, sliced into 2cm-thick rounds
1 teaspoon smoked paprika
1 garlic clove, peeled and sliced
1 x 400g can borlotti beans, drained and rinsed
1 x 400g can chopped tomatoes
1 teaspoon dried chilli flakes

for the polenta:
2 teaspoons vegetable stock powder
200g quick polenta
50g salted butter
50g freshly grated Parmesan cheese
Salt and white pepper, to taste

for the garnish:
4 spring onions, finely chopped

1   Place a medium saucepan over a medium heat and cook the chorizo for 5 minutes. Stir occasionally with a wooden spoon.

2   Add the paprika and garlic and cook for a further minute. Continue to stir.

3   Pour in the borlotti beans and the tomatoes, add the chilli flakes and gently cook for 12 minutes, uncovered. Stir occasionally.

4   Meanwhile, make the polenta. Measure out 800ml of boiling water from the kettle and pour into a large saucepan. Add the stock powder and bring to the boil. Slowly sprinkle in the polenta and whisk continuously for 1 minute, until thick. Once it has boiled for 1 minute remove from the heat and stir in the butter and the Parmesan and season with salt and pepper.

5   Season the chorizo and bean stew with salt.

6   Spoon the polenta in the centre of 4 serving plates and top with the stew.

7   Scatter over the chopped spring onions.

8   Serve hot with a nice bottle of Italian red wine.

ITALIAN SAUSAGE PATTIES

with

MASH AND ONION GRAVY

This is a quick version of sausage and mash, which I love to make with Italian sausages as they are full of delicious herbs and spices such as fennel and rosemary. Using red onion marmalade makes a quick but really flavoursome gravy.

Svizzerine di salsicce

---

serves 4

1 beef stock cube
8 Italian pork sausages
3 tablespoons olive oil
1 tablespoon plain flour
50ml red wine
6 tablespoons caramelised red onion marmalade
Salt and white pepper, to taste

for the mash:
1kg floury potatoes, e.g. King Edward or Maris Piper, peeled and cut into 3cm chunks
80ml full-fat milk
50g salted butter

1 Preheat the oven to 180°C/gas 4. Put the potatoes in a large saucepan. Cover with boiling water from the kettle, add 2 teaspoons of salt and cook for 8 minutes.

2 Meanwhile, pour 300ml of boiling water into a measuring jug and crumble in the stock cube. Mix and set aside.

3 Remove the sausages from their skins and divide each one into two. Roll the pieces into balls and flatten into a patty.

4 Heat the olive oil in a large frying pan and cook the sausage patties for 2 minutes on each side. Remove from the pan, transfer to a baking tray and cook in the oven for 5 minutes.

5 Meanwhile, add the flour to the frying pan to soak up any fat, and cook for 1 minute. Stir occasionally with a wooden spoon. Pour in the red wine and scrape all the caramelised bits from the bottom of the pan as these add real flavour to the gravy.

6 Pour the stock into the frying pan and stir continuously to prevent lumps forming. Bring to the boil, stir in the caramelised red onion marmalade and season with black pepper. Simmer gently until ready to serve.

7 Drain the potatoes, tip back into the saucepan and mash with the milk and butter. Stir well and season with salt and pepper.

8 Serve the patties with the mashed potatoes and drizzle over the gravy.

PORK

and

APPLE MEATBALLS

Pork and apples complement each other beautifully and this speedy recipe is both comforting and delicious.

Polpette di maiale e mele

---

serves 4

750g minced pork
2 eating apples
6 sage leaves, chopped
5 tablespoons olive oil
1 tablespoon cornflour
100ml soured cream
150ml hot chicken stock
3 tablespoons chopped flatleaf parsley
Salt and black pepper, to taste

for the mash:
1kg floury potatoes, e.g. King Edward or Maris Piper, peeled and cut into 3cm chunks
60g salted butter
80ml double cream

1 Put the potatoes into a large saucepan and cover with boiling water from the kettle. Add 2 teaspoons of salt and boil for 10 minutes.

2 Meanwhile, put the minced pork in a large bowl. Grate in the apples (no need to peel them: just grate down to the core). Add the sage, season with salt and pepper and mix everything together. Roll the pork mix into 12 meatballs.

3 Heat the oil in a medium frying pan and cook the meatballs for 7 minutes, turning them regularly so they are browned all over.

4 Drain the potatoes and return to the same saucepan, stir in the butter and start to mash. Add the cream and continue to mash until smooth. Season with salt and pepper.

5 Transfer the meatballs to a plate, cover with foil and set aside.

6 Mix the cornflour in a cup with 2 tablespoons cold water.

7 Add the soured cream to the frying pan used to cook the meatballs. Pour the stock over the soured cream followed by the cornflour mixture. Keep stirring with a wooden spoon while it comes to a simmer, then remove from the heat. Stir in the parsley and season with salt and pepper.

8 Serve the meatballs with the mash and spoon over the parsley sauce.

THINLY SLICED LAMB

with

WATERCRESS AND BALSAMIC VINEGAR

Tagliata means 'cut' or 'sliced' and it is the perfect family meal for sharing. It is also a great way to make meat go a little further because slicing it thinly makes it look as if there's a whole lot more than there is – a canny Italian trick! You can make this recipe using any leftover roast beef or lamb too. I suggest keeping the meat nice and rare – you get the best flavour that way. Peppery watercress and salty Pecorino are perfect with the sweet lamb meat.

Tagliata di agnello

serves 4

2 x 200g lamb rump steaks, excess fat removed
2 tablespoons olive oil
250g baby tomatoes on the vine, in small bunches
3 tablespoons balsamic vinegar
1 tablespoon redcurrant jelly
1 tablespoon salted capers, rinsed under cold water
1 tablespoon freshly chopped flatleaf parsley
100g watercress
50g Pecorino cheese
3 tablespoons extra virgin olive oil
Salt and pepper, to taste
Crusty bread, to serve

1 Preheat the oven to 200°C/gas 6 and preheat a medium frying pan over a high heat.

2 Drizzle the lamb with the olive oil and fry for 2 minutes on each side. Remove from the pan and transfer to a roasting tray with the tomatoes. Cook in the oven for 10 minutes.

3 Return the frying pan to the heat and pour in the balsamic vinegar and redcurrant jelly. Cook for 30 seconds, stirring with a wooden spoon. Stir in the capers and parsley, and season with salt and pepper. Set aside.

4 Pile the watercress onto a large serving platter. Use a peeler to shave the Pecorino cheese on top of the watercress. Drizzle over the extra virgin olive oil and season with salt and pepper.

5 Remove the lamb from the oven, and leave to rest for 2 minutes on a plate at room temperature. Season with salt and pepper.

6 Place the roasted tomatoes around the serving platter.

7 Thinly slice the lamb, place on top of the watercress and drizzle over the balsamic and redcurrant sauce.

8 Serve immediately with crusty bread.

LAMB PITTA POCKETS
with
MASCARPONE DRESSING

Little lamb patties stuffed inside warm pitta bread and crammed full of salad make an amazing alternative to a burger. There is far less bread and they are almost easier to eat as the natural pocket shape helps keep them together. My kids love these as they can make their own, filling it up with as much or as little of each ingredient as they like. The minted mascarpone is fantastic with the lamb!

Portafogli di pane con agnello e mascarpone

serves 4

500g minced lamb
2 tablespoons sweet chilli sauce
2 tablespoons chopped chives
3 tablespoons olive oil
4 pitta breads: either white or wholemeal
110g bag of lettuce leaves
4 large plum tomatoes, sliced lengthways
Salt and white pepper, to taste

for the mascarpone dressing:
8 tablespoons mascarpone cheese
Juice of ½ lemon
1 tablespoon freshly chopped mint

1 Put the minced lamb in a large bowl with the sweet chilli sauce and chopped chives. Season with salt and pepper. Mix together and divide the mixture into 12 balls. Gently flatten the balls into patties.

2 Heat the olive oil in a large frying pan and fry the patties for 3 minutes on each side. Transfer onto some kitchen paper to absorb any excess oil and set aside.

3 Mix together the mascarpone, lemon juice and mint in a medium bowl. Add a splash of water to the mascarpone dressing to loosen it slightly so it has the consistency of mayonnaise. Set aside.

4 Heat the pitta bread in a toaster until warm; do not overheat them otherwise they will become hard and impossible to open like a pocket.

5 Carefully split open the pitta breads and fill the pocket with lettuce, tomatoes, lamb patties and mascarpone dressing.

6 Enjoy with a cold beer or a glass of juice for the kids.

LAMB KEBABS

with

TOMATO AND FETA CHEESE SALSA

I like kebabs that have a bit of texture to them and therefore diced leg of lamb is a great choice for this recipe. If you like the meat really tender you can use fillet of lamb, although this costs a lot more and is less 'lamby'. Oregano gives the meat a wonderful flavour – the taste of the Mediterranean.

Spiedini di gamba d'agnello

---

serves 4

600g leg of lamb, cut into 2cm chunks
2 tablespoons olive oil
1 teaspoon dried oregano
2 red onions

for the salsa:
250g cherry tomatoes
2 tablespoons mint leaves
150g feta cheese
2 tablespoons olive oil
Salt and black pepper, to taste

8 wooden skewers, soaked in cold water

1 Heat a griddle pan over a high heat.

2 Put the lamb in a large bowl, drizzle over the oil and sprinkle in the dried oregano. Season with salt and pepper, mix well and set aside.

3 Peel and cut the red onions into 8 wedges. Try to cut them through the root (the small circular non-layered part at the base of the onion), as this will hold the layers of the onion together, ensuring that each wedge maintains its shape.

4 Thread the lamb and onions onto the skewers and cook on the griddle pan for 8 minutes. Turn the skewers every 2 minutes to ensure that all sides are cooked.

5 Meanwhile, cut the cherry tomatoes in half and put in a bowl. Roughly slice the mint leaves and add to the tomatoes. Crumble over the feta cheese, drizzle with the oil and season with black pepper. Gently mix together.

6 Once the kebabs are cooked, remove from the griddle and serve with the tomato and feta cheese salsa.

SPICY LAMB MEATBALLS

with

ITALIAN FLATBREADS AND QUICK TOMATO SAUCE

The best-known flatbreads are pittas, tortillas or Turkish flatbreads that you can pick up in most supermarkets and specialist shops, but now, I'm pleased to say, you can also find lots of Italian flatbreads. They tend to be much richer than the other flatbreads as they are usually made with extra virgin olive oil. If you can't get hold of them, brush any flatbread with a little extra virgin olive oil and warm through in the oven.

Polpette piccanti con pomodorini

serves 4

500g minced lamb
2 garlic cloves, peeled
1 teaspoon dried chilli flakes
3 tablespoons olive oil, plus extra for brushing
4 large Italian flatbreads, such as piadina or schiacciata
140g bag of rocket leaves
Salt and black pepper, to taste

for the tomato sauce:
3 tablespoons olive oil
300g cherry tomatoes
3 tablespoons white wine vinegar
3 tablespoons caster sugar
10 basil leaves

1   Preheat the oven to 180°C/gas 4.

2   Put the minced lamb in a large bowl and finely grate in the garlic. Season with salt and the chilli flakes and mix together. Divide into 20 pieces and roll into small balls.

3   Pour the olive oil in a large frying pan over a medium heat. Cook the meatballs for 8 minutes, turning them regularly so that they brown all over.

4   Meanwhile, brush the flatbreads with a little olive oil (preferably extra virgin) and wrap them in a pile in foil. Put in the oven to warm through.

5   To make the sauce, heat the oil in a medium frying pan and add the tomatoes. Cook for 2 minutes, stirring occasionally with a wooden spoon. Add the vinegar and sugar and continue to cook for a further 2 minutes. Stir in the basil leaves and set aside.

6   Place the meatballs in the middle of a large serving plate surrounded by the tomato sauce and rocket leaves.

7   Serve immediately with the warm Italian flatbreads.

LAMB MEATBALLS

with

SPICY TOMATO SAUCE AND HERBY COUSCOUS

The red wine reduction in this sauce gives a warm and rich flavour which can be achieved surprisingly quickly. The chilli flakes add a subtle spice that works beautifully with the freshness of the parsley and sweetness of the apricots in the couscous.

Polpettine di agnello

serves 4

150ml red wine
500g minced lamb
1 garlic clove, peeled
1 tablespoon dried oregano
4 tablespoons olive oil
½ teaspoon dried chilli flakes
1 x 400g can chopped tomatoes

for the couscous:
200g couscous
2 tablespoons vegetable stock powder
3 tablespoons extra virgin olive oil
50g dried apricots, chopped
10 small basil leaves
3 tablespoons freshly chopped flatleaf parsley
Salt and black pepper, to taste

1   Pour the red wine into a small saucepan and bring to the boil. Reduce the heat and gently simmer for 8 minutes. Stir occasionally with a wooden spoon.

2   Meanwhile, put the couscous in a large heatproof bowl, add the stock powder and pour over 500ml boiling water from the kettle. Cover with clingfilm and set aside.

3   Put the minced lamb in a large bowl and grate the garlic over the top. Add the oregano and season well with salt and pepper. Mix together and roll into 20 small balls.

4   Heat the olive oil in a large frying pan and cook the meatballs for 5 minutes, turning them regularly so that they brown all over.

5   Add the chilli flakes and tomatoes to the frying pan with the tomatoes and pour in the reduced red wine. Stir together and cook for a further 8 minutes, stirring occasionally.

6   Use a fork to loosen the couscous grains, pour in the extra virgin olive oil and carefully stir in the chopped apricots, basil and parsley. Season with salt and pepper.

7   Serve the meatballs with the spicy sauce on a bed of herby couscous.

LAMB CHOPS

---

with

ROASTED VEGETABLES AND HOMEMADE MINT SAUCE

Lamb and mint are a match made in culinary heaven, and to make my mint sauce Italian I use balsamic instead of malt or white wine vinegar, as it cuts through the fattiness of the lamb chops perfectly. If you want to achieve this in 20 minutes, don't worry about cutting the vegetables precisely – they can be nice and rustic.

Costolette d'agnello con salsa alla menta

---

serves 4

200g cherry tomatoes on the vine
2 courgettes, cut into 1cm rounds
2 yellow peppers, halved,
deseeded and cut into 1cm slices
Bunch of spring onions, trimmed
and roughly sliced
5 tablespoons olive oil
4 sprigs of rosemary
8 lamb chops

for the mint sauce:
2 tablespoons balsamic vinegar
1 tablespoon caster sugar
3 tablespoons olive oil
10 mint leaves
Salt and black pepper, to taste

1 Preheat the oven to 220°C/gas 7.

2 Cut the tomatoes into small bunches and place on a large baking tray along with all the veg. Drizzle over 3 tablespoons of olive oil, add the rosemary sprigs and season with salt and pepper. Cook in the oven for 15 minutes. Every 5 minutes remove the tray from the oven, stir the veg and continue to cook.

3 Meanwhile, heat 2 tablespoons of oil in a large frying pan. Cook the lamb chops for 4 minutes on each side. Transfer the chops to a plate and season with salt and pepper. Cover with foil and set aside.

4 To make the mint sauce, mix together the balsamic vinegar, sugar and the olive oil. Finely chop the mint and stir into the sauce. Season with salt and pepper.

5 Pile the roasted vegetables in the middle of 4 serving plates and arrange the chops on top. Drizzle over the mint sauce and serve. You could also try this with my fruity bulgar wheat (see page 79).

SPICED LAMB CHOPS

with

SWEET POTATOES

Tasty lamb flavoured with thyme, lemon and paprika and served with caramelised sweet potatoes – what's not to like? You need to get a wiggle on with the prep of the potatoes for this recipe: the high natural sugar content of sweet potatoes means they cook and caramelise much faster than ordinary potatoes. Make sure you brown the edges of the potatoes to get a beautiful caramel flavour.

Costolette di agnello con patate dolci

serves 4

8 lamb chops
3 tablespoons olive oil
Juice of 1 lemon
1 teaspoon thyme leaves
½ teaspoon smoked paprika
Salt, to taste

for the sweet potatoes:
3 large sweet potatoes, washed and cut into 1cm cubes
3 tablespoons olive oil
Pinch of cayenne pepper
1 tablespoon fresh rosemary leaves

1 Preheat the oven to 220°C/gas 7.

2 Put the potatoes on a large baking tray. Drizzle over the oil and sprinkle with the cayenne pepper and salt. Add the rosemary, toss everything together and roast in the oven for 15 minutes. Shake the baking tray every 5 minutes during roasting.

3 Preheat a large frying pan over a high heat.

4 Meanwhile, place the lamb chops on a plate and drizzle over the oil. Squeeze over the lemon juice and sprinkle with thyme leaves and paprika, ensuring the chops are well coated. Cook in the frying pan for 4 minutes on each side.

5 Transfer the chops to a plate, season with salt and set aside to rest for 1 minute.

6 Serve the lamb chops with the caramelised sweet potatoes and a salad of your choice.

7 For a more substantial meal, serve with some green beans and polenta.

LAMB STEAKS

with

WARM BABY GEMS AND PEAS

Cooking lettuce may seem a little odd but many of the top restaurants have been doing it for years. Lettuces like baby gems become soft and sweet as they cook and make a perfect match for the peas and parsley.

Agnello con pisellini

serves 4

4 lamb steaks
3 tablespoons olive oil
25g salted butter, plus 1 teaspoon softened butter
1 shallot, peeled and finely sliced
4 baby gem lettuces, quartered
300ml hot chicken stock
1 teaspoon plain flour
200g frozen peas, defrosted
2 tablespoons freshly chopped flatleaf parsley
4 tablespoons crème fraîche, to serve
Salt and black pepper, to taste

1   Preheat the grill to moderate.

2   Put the lamb steaks on a grill tray and drizzle over 2 tablespoons of olive oil. Cook under the grill for 6 minutes on each side.

3   Heat the butter and the remaining oil in a medium frying pan. Cook the shallot for 2 minutes until soft and translucent. Stir occasionally with a wooden spoon.

4   Add the baby gems to the frying pan, cut-side down. Cook for 2 minutes. Pour in the stock and bring to a simmer.

5   Mix together the softened butter and flour. Whisk into the frying pan and simmer for 2 minutes. Add the peas and continue to cook for a further 2 minutes.

6   Remove the lamb from the grill and leave to rest for 2 minutes on a plate at room temperature. Season with salt and pepper.

7   Meanwhile, stir the parsley into the frying pan with the lettuce and peas.

8   Serve the peas and baby gems in deep, wide bowls with the grilled steaks on top and a spoonful of crème fraîche to garnish.

LAMB CUTLETS

with

FENNEL SALAD AND HONEY SAUCE

Lamb cutlets are my favourite cut of lamb and to my mind there is only one way to cook them: fast and medium-rare. I learned this way of serving them when I was training in catering college and I remember that I was very impressed with the smooth flavours. If you prefer, you can substitute the honey with maple syrup – it works just as well.

Costolette di agnello con miele e finocchio

serves 4

4 tablespoons olive oil
8–12 lamb cutlets, preferably French-trimmed (ask your butcher to do this for you)
3 tablespoons fresh rosemary leaves
3 tablespoons runny honey
12 thin slices of pancetta
Salt and black pepper, to taste

for the fennel salad:
100g pitted Kalamata olives in oil or brine, drained
2 large fennel bulbs, finely sliced
1 tablespoon runny honey
4 tablespoons extra virgin olive oil
Juice of ½ lemon
2 tablespoons freshly chopped flatleaf parsley

1 To make the fennel salad, halve the olives and put them in a large bowl with the fennel slices. Drizzle over the honey and extra virgin olive oil. Squeeze in the lemon juice and add the parsley. Season with salt and pepper, mix well and set aside.

2 Heat the olive oil in a large frying pan over a high heat.

3 Fry the lamb cutlets with the rosemary in the hot oil for 2 minutes on each side. Transfer to a plate, season with salt and pepper and cover with foil to keep warm.

4 Drizzle the honey into the frying pan and stir with a wooden spoon for 1 minute over a low heat. Season with black pepper and set aside.

5 Pile the fennel salad into the middle of 4 serving plates and place the slices of pancetta on top. Arrange the cutlets around the salad and drizzle over the honey dressing.

6 Serve immediately with lots of warm Italian bread or my New Potato Salad with Red Onions and Capers (see page 201).

LAMB CUTLETS

coated with

PARMA HAM AND PARMESAN

I honestly can't remember how many times I have cooked this recipe. It is one of my wife's favourites and as a good husband I was born to please her, over and over again. You can substitute the Parmesan with Pecorino if you prefer and sliced pancetta works just as well as the Parma ham.

Costolette impanate

---

serves 4

50g sliced Parma ham, finely chopped
80g toasted fine breadcrumbs
3 tablespoons freshly grated Parmesan cheese
12 lamb cutlets, preferably French-trimmed (ask your butcher to do this for you)
2 large eggs, beaten into a medium bowl
6 tablespoons olive oil
Warm bread, to serve

for the salad:
140g rocket leaves
20 cherry tomatoes, halved
3 tablespoons extra virgin olive oil
3 tablespoons balsamic vinegar
Salt and black pepper, to taste

1 Mix together the Parma ham with the breadcrumbs and Parmesan cheese in a large bowl. Set aside.

2 Dip each cutlet first into the beaten eggs and immediately coat with the breadcrumb mixture. Press the lamb firmly into the breadcrumb mixture so it coats the cutlets evenly.

3 Heat the oil in a large frying pan over a medium heat.

4 Cook the cutlets in the hot oil for 3 minutes on each side.

5 Transfer the cutlets to some kitchen paper to absorb any excess oil. Season with salt and pepper.

6 Meanwhile, put the rocket leaves in a large bowl with the cherry tomatoes. Drizzle over the extra virgin olive oil and balsamic vinegar. Season with salt and pepper and mix well.

7 Serve the cutlets with the beautiful rocket salad and lots of warm bread on the side. It would also go rather well with the Carrots and Almonds with Fresh Mint and Chilli (see page 23).

CANNON OF LAMB

with

CAPERS AND ROSEMARY

The cannon of lamb is the fillet; it is very low in fat, just like fillet of beef, but it is also extremely tender. You really need to serve this cut nice and pink to get the best out of it. The flavour is mild so it goes well with stronger-tasting ingredients like capers and rosemary, both favourites with Italians.

Filetto di agnello con capperi

serves 4

400g new potatoes
4 x 175g cannon of lamb fillets
2 tablespoons olive oil
200g green beans
1 tablespoon rosemary leaves
150ml white wine
2 tablespoons capers in vinegar, drained
1 tablespoon freshly chopped flatleaf parsley
30g salted butter
Juice of ½ lemon
Salt and black pepper, to taste

1 Preheat a frying pan over a high heat.

2 Put the potatoes in a medium saucepan and cover with boiling water from the kettle. Add 1 teaspoon of salt and boil for 8 minutes.

3 Roll the lamb fillets in the olive oil and cook in the frying pan for 3–4 minutes until golden brown. Turn the fillets regularly so that they brown all over. Remove the pan from the heat, transfer the lamb to a plate and set aside.

4 Use a slotted spoon to scoop the potatoes out of the boiling water and put in a large bowl to keep warm.

5 Add the beans to the boiling water and boil for 2 minutes.

6 Meanwhile, return the frying pan to the heat and add the rosemary. Cook for 2 minutes, stirring with a wooden spoon. Pour in the wine, stir and cook for a further 2 minutes, stirring continuously. Add the capers, parsley and 20g butter. Season with salt and pepper and set aside.

7 Meanwhile, drain the beans, tip them back into the same saucepan and add the remaining butter. Squeeze over the lemon juice and season with salt and pepper. Set aside.

8 Carve each piece of lamb into 1cm thick slices and serve alongside the potatoes and beans. Drizzle over the rich wine sauce and serve immediately.

LAMB MEDALLIONS

with

HAZELNUT DRESSING

Texture is so important when it comes to food – it can transform a dish from dull to amazing in minutes and nuts are a great way of achieving this. Italian cooks use hazelnuts in a vast array of dishes, savoury and sweet, from salads to desserts. If you prefer you can substitute the hazelnuts with walnuts.

Medaglioni con salsina di noci

serves 4

400g small new potatoes
4 x 175g fillets of lamb
4 tablespoons olive oil
1 teaspoon Dijon mustard
1 tablespoon white wine vinegar
2 tablespoons hazelnut oil
200g green beans, cut into 2cm lengths
50g chopped hazelnuts
1 tablespoon freshly chopped mint, to serve
Salt and black pepper, to taste

1   Preheat the oven to 200°C/gas 6.

2   Put the potatoes in a medium saucepan and cover with boiling water from the kettle. Add 1 teaspoon of salt and boil for 7 minutes.

3   Put the lamb fillet on a baking tray and drizzle over half the olive oil. Roast in the oven for 8 minutes. After 4 minutes of cooking, turn the lamb so it browns all over.

4   Whisk together the mustard, vinegar and hazelnut oil in a small bowl. Season with salt and pepper and set aside.

5   Drain the potatoes, cut in half and put in a large bowl.

6   Remove the lamb from the oven and transfer to a plate, season with salt and pepper and cover with foil to keep warm.

7   Heat the remaining olive oil in a large frying pan and add the drained potatoes. Fry for 1 minute before adding the beans. Continue to fry for a further 3 minutes until the beans are just cooked, stirring occasionally with a wooden spoon.

8   Remove the potatoes and beans from the heat, pour in the dressing and stir in the chopped hazelnuts. Slice the lamb in 2cm thick medallions. Arrange the beans and potatoes in the centre of a large serving platter and place the lamb on top. Sprinkle over the freshly chopped mint and serve.

QUICK LAMB STEW

with

BABY NEW POTATOES

Stews normally take hours to cook because the cuts of meat traditionally used are the larger muscles that the animal used most; therefore, they taste the best but are tougher, requiring long, slow cooking. This stew is a quick variation but still has all the flavour of a traditional version.

Stufato d'agnello

serves 4

400g baby new potatoes
2 carrots, peeled and cut into 1cm cubes
4 tablespoons olive oil
500g leg of lamb, cut into 2cm cubes
1 tablespoon plain flour
100ml red wine
500ml hot beef or lamb stock
2 tablespoons mint jelly
150g frozen peas, defrosted
1 tablespoon freshly chopped mint
Salt and black pepper, to taste
Warm crusty bread, to serve

1   Put the potatoes in a medium saucepan and cover with boiling water from the kettle. Add 1 teaspoon of salt and cook for 7 minutes.

2   Cook the carrots for 1 minute with the potatoes (add to the pan for the last minute of cooking time). Drain the lot and set aside.

3   Meanwhile, heat the oil in a large frying pan and fry the lamb for 8 minutes. Stir occasionally with a wooden spoon to ensure that the pieces brown all over. Remove from the frying pan and set aside.

4   Add the flour to the frying pan, stir well and cook for 1 minute. Pour in the wine and bring to the boil, still stirring. Pour in the stock and continue to cook for 3 minutes, stirring continuously.

5   Return the lamb to the frying pan with the mint jelly. Stir well and cook gently for 6 minutes, stirring occasionally.

6   Add the potatoes, carrots, peas and fresh mint. Simmer for a further minute, season with salt and pepper and serve immediately with lots of warm crusty bread to mop up the delicious sauce.

LAMB, SPINACH
and
GORGONZOLA PIE

The great thing about minced meat is that it cooks much quicker than larger cuts, so you have time to make this delicious lamb pie within 20 minutes. Rather like a Greek kotopita, it uses filo pastry, which takes a matter of minutes to cook, unlike the more traditional pie pastries such as shortcrust or puff.

Torta salata con agnello e Gorgonzola

serves 4

3 tablespoons olive oil
2 tablespoons fresh rosemary leaves, finely chopped
500g minced lamb
2 garlic cloves, peeled
400g baby spinach leaves
4 large sheets of filo pastry
50g salted butter, melted
200g Gorgonzola cheese, chilled
Salt and black pepper, to taste

1 Preheat the oven to 220°C/gas 7.

2 Heat the oil in a large frying pan with the rosemary, add the minced lamb and cook for 3 minutes. Stir occasionally with a wooden spoon to break the mince up.

3 Grate the garlic on top of the meat and cook for a further 2 minutes.

4 Add the spinach and continue to cook for 3 minutes, stirring occasionally. Season with salt and pepper and set aside.

5 Lay one sheet of filo pastry onto a chopping board. Brush with a little of the melted butter and place in a 20cm cake tin, letting the edges of the pastry hang over the sides. Repeat with the remaining sheets until the base and sides of the tin are covered and there is a lot of overhang.

6 Spoon the mince and spinach mixture into the middle of the tin and crumble over the Gorgonzola. Cover the top of the pie with the overhanging pastry.

7 Brush the top with melted butter and grind over some black pepper. Cook in the middle of the oven for 10 minutes.

8 Serve hot with your favourite salad on the side.

BUILD YOUR OWN BEEF BRUSCHETTA

Half the pleasure of food is being able to enjoy it with your friends and family. I love dishes that can be placed in the centre of the table and everybody helps themselves. It's the most social form of eating and it means I'm not stuck in the kitchen! This recipe cooks the beef from scratch, but if you have any leftover roast beef from a Sunday roast by all means use that.

Bruschetta fai da te

serves 4

300g steak, cut of your choice
3 tablespoons olive oil
1 ciabatta, cut into 2cm thick slices
200g cherry tomatoes, halved
1 garlic clove, peeled and halved
6 tablespoons extra virgin olive oil
6 basil leaves, torn
150g ricotta cheese
Small bunch of mixed herbs, such as parsley, dill or chives, finely chopped
Zest and juice of 1 unwaxed lemon
8 sun-dried tomatoes in oil, drained
80g pitted mixed olives in oil or brine, drained
50g Parmesan cheese
150g rocket leaves
Salt and black pepper, to taste

1. Preheat a griddle pan and put a frying pan over a high heat. Drizzle the steak with a little of the olive oil and cook in the hot frying pan for 2 minutes on each side. Transfer to a plate and season with salt and pepper. Cover with foil and set aside.

2. Brush the slices of ciabatta with the rest of the olive oil. Place on the griddle pan and cook until crispy and golden on both sides.

3. Put the cherry tomatoes in a bowl and finely grate over one half of the garlic. Pour in half the extra virgin olive oil, season with salt and pepper and stir in the basil leaves. Set aside.

4. Put the ricotta cheese in a separate bowl and stir in the herbs and lemon zest. Season with salt and pepper and set aside.

5. Rub the griddled bread with the remaining half garlic clove and place on a large serving board. Arrange the sun-dried tomatoes and olives around the board then use a swivel-head potato peeler to create a pile of Parmesan shavings.

6. Put the rocket leaves in a bowl and dress with the lemon juice, the remaining extra virgin olive oil, salt and pepper. Make a pile of dressed leaves on the serving board or serve separately.

7. Slice the steak thinly with a long sharp knife and pile onto the serving board.

8. Place the serving board in the centre of the table with the bowls of tomatoes and ricotta and let everybody enjoy making their own tasty bruschetta.

BEEF SALAD

with

LEMON, CHILLI AND CHIVES

This dish combines simple flavours so make sure you buy good-quality ingredients – the best you can afford. Fillet of beef is so tender it is perfect for eating 'blue' by quickly searing it on all sides in a hot pan while the centre stays beautifully rare. If, however, you are not a fan of really rare meat, preheat the oven to 200°C/gas 6, sear your steak, and then pop it into the oven for 8 minutes to cook a little more.

Insalata rustica

serves 4

300g beef fillet
4 tablespoons olive oil
1 red chilli, halved, deseeded and finely chopped
280g chargrilled artichokes in oil, drained and halved
Juice of 1 lemon
50g pine nuts
70g mixed salad leaves
2 tablespoons chopped chives
3 tablespoons extra virgin olive oil
Salt and black pepper, to taste

1   Preheat a large frying pan until very hot.

2   Put the beef on a large flat plate and drizzle over the olive oil, season with salt and pepper and make sure that it is seasoned all over. Put the beef in the frying pan and fry for 3 minutes on each side.

3   Remove the pan from the heat and transfer the meat to rest on a plate, covered with foil to keep warm.

4   Add the chilli and artichokes to the beef pan and squeeze over a little of the lemon juice. Stir and set aside.

5   Put the pine nuts in a small frying pan and toast over a medium heat until golden brown – take care as they burn really easily.

6   Use a really sharp knife to slice the beef in 0.5cm thick slices and arrange on a large serving plate.

7   Scatter over the warm artichokes and chilli then top with the salad leaves and toasted pine nuts.

8   Squeeze over the remaining lemon juice. Top with the chopped chives and finally drizzle with the extra virgin olive oil. Serve with warm crusty bread.

BRESAOLA AND QUAIL'S EGG SALAD

This is one of the fastest salads that you can throw together. It's almost cheating as lots of it is pre-cooked and bought ready-prepared, but when time is tight it's good to have a helping hand. Bresaola is an Italian speciality – salted beef that is air-dried for 2–3 months, so even if you had an hour to cook you couldn't make this yourself!

Bresaola con uova di quaglie

serves 4

12 quail's eggs
125g fine asparagus tips
2 tablespoons olive oil
150g sliced Bresaola
1 tablespoon tarragon leaves
100g mayonnaise
Juice of ½ lemon
Salt and black pepper, to taste

1 Put the quail's eggs in a small saucepan and cover with boiling water from the kettle. Boil for 5 minutes. Put the saucepan under cold running water for 2 minutes. Peel the eggs and set aside.

2 Preheat a griddle pan over a high heat.

3 Put the asparagus on a plate and drizzle over the olive oil, season with salt and pepper and mix well. Cook on the griddle pan for 3–4 minutes, turning occasionally. Transfer to a plate and set aside.

4 Arrange the Bresaola slices on 4 serving plates. Halve the quail's eggs and place on top of the meat. Share the asparagus between the plates.

5 Chop the tarragon and put into a bowl. Mix in the mayonnaise and lemon juice, adding just enough cold water to create a runny dressing. Season with salt and pepper and drizzle the dressing over the salad.

THE ULTIMATE STEAK ROLL

Nothing beats a soft ciabatta roll that is flavour-packed and filled with so many ingredients that it is difficult and messy to cut! This recipe is another great way to make a good piece of steak go a little further.

Panino fantastico

serves 2

1 x 250g rump or sirloin steak
2 tablespoons olive oil
2 individual ciabatta rolls, halved
3 tablespoons mayonnaise
2 tablespoons good-quality ready-made pesto
1 ripe avocado
2 handfuls of mixed salad leaves
4 sun-dried tomatoes in oil, drained
Salt and black pepper, to taste

1 Put a frying pan over a high heat.

2 Rub the steak with olive oil and cook in the hot frying pan for 2 minutes on each side.

3 Transfer the steak to a plate and season with salt and pepper. Cover with foil and set aside.

4 Place the ciabatta halves, cut-side down, in the pan you cooked the steaks in – as they toast they soak up all the steak juices until they start to go crispy.

5 Meanwhile, mix the mayonnaise with the pesto and season with black pepper. Halve the avocado, carefully remove the stone and skin, and cut into thick slices.

6 Remove the bread from the pan and spread both halves of each roll with the pesto mayo. Top the bottom half with salad leaves and avocado.

7 Using a sharp long knife, cut the steak into thin strips. Place the steak on top of the avocado, top each one with a couple of sun-dried tomatoes and sandwich with the ciabatta top. Enjoy hot and prepare to get messy!

BEEF LOLLIPOPS

with

SPICY TOMATO DIPPING SAUCE

Meatballs are often a main course but my kids love them without the pasta, served on little wooden skewers so that they look like lollipops — perfect for dipping into a spicy tomato sauce. They make a family-friendly starter as they are fun to eat. If you are making them for the kids, just watch the amount of chilli you add but if you like it hot, go for it!

Lecca lecca di manzo con salsa piccante

serves 6

50g fresh breadcrumbs
50ml semi-skimmed or
full-fat milk
4 tablespoons olive oil
500g minced beef
1 teaspoon fresh oregano leaves,
chopped
1 teaspoon Dijon mustard

for the spicy tomato sauce:
2 tablespoons olive oil
2 garlic cloves, peeled and sliced
300ml passata
Pinch of dried chilli flakes
1 tablespoon sweet chilli sauce
12 fresh basil leaves
Salt, to taste

1 Put the breadcrumbs in a small bowl and pour over the milk. Leave for 2 minutes for the milk to soak into the breadcrumbs. Set aside.

2 Heat 2 tablespoons of the olive oil in a medium saucepan. Add the garlic and fry for 30 seconds, pour in the passata and add the chilli flakes. Cook gently for 10 minutes. Stir occasionally with a wooden spoon.

3 Meanwhile, place the minced beef in a large bowl. Add the oregano, mustard and soaked breadcrumbs. Season with salt and mix together.

4 Roll the mix to make 24 mini meatballs.

5 Heat the remaining olive oil in a large frying pan and fry the meatballs for 7 minutes, until brown all over.

6 Add the sweet chilli sauce and basil leaves to the tomato sauce. Season with salt and stir.

7 Serve the meatballs on small wooden skewers with the spicy tomato sauce on the side. Enjoy!

ITALIAN-STYLE CHEESE BURGERS

with

COLESLAW CUPS

Burgers are a great Friday night supper, perfect for the whole family. I love using mozzarella to melt on top of the beef patties as it goes so beautifully stringy

Svizzerine di manzo con insalatina

serves 4

500g minced beef
1 teaspoon English mustard
4 good-quality burger buns
1 x 125g mozzarella ball, drained
and cut into 4 thick slices
4 tablespoons tomato chutney,
to serve

for the coleslaw cups:
1 tablespoon wholegrain mustard
6 tablespoons mayonnaise
Juice of ½ lemon
2 carrots, peeled and grated
1 fennel bulb, grated
¼ red cabbage, finely chopped
2 baby gem lettuces
Salt and white pepper, to taste

1 Preheat the oven to 150°C/gas 2 and put a griddle pan over a high heat.

2 Mix the minced beef and mustard in a large bowl. Try not to crush it with your hands too much as this makes the burgers too dense. Season well with salt and pepper and divide the mix into four. Shape into burgers about 2.5cm thick. Put the burgers onto the griddle pan and cook for 4 minutes on one side.

3 Meanwhile, put the buns on a baking tray and pop them into the oven to warm through.

4 Mix together the wholegrain mustard, mayonnaise and lemon juice in a large bowl and season with salt and pepper. Add the carrots and fennel to the mayonnaise mixture. Stir everything together and set aside.

5 Turn the burgers over and top each one with a slice of mozzarella. Continue to cook for 3 minutes.

6 Mix the cabbage into the coleslaw mixture. Break the baby gem lettuce into individual leaves and fill each one with some of the coleslaw.

7 Remove the buns from the oven and cut in half. Place a burger on the bottom half of each bun, then top the melted mozzarella with some tomato chutney and serve alongside the lettuce coleslaw cups.

SPICY BEEF LETTUCE CUPS

I don't often use ready-made sauces like tomato ketchup in my cooking but this adds sweetness to a hot and spicy dish. It's fun to put everything on the table and let the family tuck in and fill their own cups.

Coppette di manzo piccanti

serves 6

4 tablespoons olive oil
6 spring onions, finely chopped
1 hot red chilli, halved, deseeded and finely chopped
1 teaspoon fennel seeds, crushed
500g minced beef
2 tablespoons tomato ketchup
50ml hot beef stock
2 tablespoons freshly chopped flatleaf parsley
2 baby gem lettuces
100ml natural yogurt
40g Pecorino cheese, grated
Salt, to taste

1 Heat the oil in a large frying pan and gently fry the spring onions, chilli and fennel seeds for 30 seconds. Stir with a wooden spoon.

2 Add the minced beef and continue to fry for 10 minutes, breaking it up with a wooden spoon as it cooks.

3 Stir in the tomato ketchup and beef stock. Season with salt.

4 Remove from the heat and stir in the parsley.

5 Break the baby gem lettuces into individual leaves and place on a large serving plate. Fill each leaf cup with a little of the mince mixture and top with a spoonful of natural yogurt and a little Pecorino cheese – or let everyone do this themselves.

6 Serve with plenty of cold beer on the side for the adults and cold soft drinks for the kids.

BALSAMIC-GLAZED BEEF SKEWERS

I always have a bottle of good-quality balsamic vinegar in the cupboard as it is perfect for salad dressings and marinades. Buy the best that you can afford, that way you will enjoy its intense flavour rather than just a strong acidity. Not only does balsamic give a wonderful flavour to this recipe, its acidity also tenderises the meat.

Spiedini di manzo

serves 4

50ml good-quality balsamic vinegar
3 tablespoons runny honey
2 garlic cloves, peeled and finely chopped
600g rump steak, cut into 2cm cubes
1 yellow pepper, halved and deseeded
1 red pepper, halved and deseeded
1 courgette

for the egg-fried rice:
40g salted butter
2 x 250g packets of ready-cooked basmati rice
2 eggs, beaten
4 tablespoons freshly chopped flatleaf parsley, plus extra to garnish
Salt and black pepper, to taste

8 wooden skewers, soaked in cold water

1   Preheat a griddle pan over a high heat.

2   In a large bowl, mix together the balsamic vinegar, honey and garlic. Add the diced beef and mix well.

3   Cut the peppers into 2cm cubes and the courgettes into 0.5cm thick rounds.

4   Thread the meat, peppers and courgettes onto the skewers in random order aiming to distribute the ingredients evenly and place them on the griddle pan.

5   Cook for 6 minutes, turning occasionally and brushing them with the marinade.

6   Transfer the skewers to a plate and season with salt and pepper. Cover with foil to keep warm.

7   Melt the butter in a wok or a large frying pan and stir in the rice. Add a splash of water and cook for 2 minutes until hot.

8   Push the rice to one side and pour in the beaten eggs. Use a wooden spoon to scramble the eggs for 30 seconds before stirring in the rice and parsley. Season with salt and pepper.

9   Divide the rice between 4 serving plates and place the beef skewers on top. Serve immediately with a little more parsley sprinkled on top.

RARE ROAST BEEF

with

MINTY POTATO SALAD

This is a delicious salad. I love the combination of the cold dressing and salad with the warm beef and potatoes. If you have any leftover beef from your Sunday roast this is a great way to use it up – you'll have a meal in moments.

Insalata di manzo e patate

serves 4

300g small waxy new potatoes
8 mint leaves
400g beef fillet
2 tablespoons olive oil
8 tablespoons mayonnaise
1 small garlic clove, peeled
1 avocado
10 radishes, quartered
175g chargrilled artichokes in oil, drained and quartered
6 spring onions, finely chopped
Salt and white pepper, to taste

1 Preheat the oven to 200°C/gas 6. Put the potatoes and half of the mint in a medium saucepan, cover with boiling water from the kettle, add 1 teaspoon of salt and cook for 10 minutes.

2 Meanwhile, put a frying pan with an ovenproof handle over a high heat.

3 Rub the beef with the oil and put in the hot frying pan. Sear on all sides until browned, and then transfer to the oven to cook for 8 minutes.

4 Put the mayonnaise in a bowl and finely grate in the garlic clove. Chop the remaining mint leaves and add to the mayo. Add a little water to create a runny dressing and season with salt and pepper. Set aside.

5 Drain the potatoes and leave to cool.

6 Transfer the beef from the oven to a plate and season with salt and pepper. Cover with foil and set aside to rest at room temperature.

7 Meanwhile, halve the avocado and remove the stone. Peel off the skin and cut the flesh into rough chunks. Halve the cooled potatoes.

8 Use a long sharp knife to cut the beef into thin slices. Arrange them over a platter and scatter the prepared radishes, artichokes and avocado on top. Drizzle over the mayo dressing and sprinkle over the chopped spring onions.

ROAST RIB OF BEEF

with

CREAMY LEEKS AND CANNELLINI BEANS

Bistecca con crema di porri e cannellini

Roast rib of beef seems an unlikely dish to cook in 20 minutes. However, if you can get hold of single-bone ribs they are just like cooking an extra-thick steak, but with the added flavour from the bone. Rib of beef is deliciously tender meat and perfect eaten rare. It's typically Italian to use cannellini beans – I think their flavour and texture is brilliant with a juicy steak.

serves 4

1 'on the bone' rib of beef, about
6cm thick
2 tablespoons olive oil
4 sprigs of rosemary
30g salted butter
2 leeks, trimmed and cut into
0.5cm rounds
1 tablespoon thyme leaves
1 garlic clove, peeled
50ml white wine
2 x 400g cans cannellini beans,
drained and rinsed
200ml double cream
100ml hot chicken stock
Salt and white pepper, to taste

1. Preheat the oven to 220°C/gas 7. Put a large ovenproof frying pan over a high heat.

2. Rub the beef with half the oil and cook in the hot frying pan for 2 minutes on each side. Add the rosemary to the pan and transfer it to the oven to roast for 12 minutes.

3. Meanwhile, melt the butter with the remaining olive oil in a medium frying pan. Add the leeks and fry for 2 minutes. Stir occasionally with a wooden spoon.

4. Add the thyme leaves and grate in the garlic. Mix everything together and fry for a further minute. Pour in the white wine and continue to cook for 1 minute.

5. Add the cannellini beans to the frying pan. Stir well before pouring in the double cream and stock. Gently cook for 4 minutes and stir occasionally.

6. Remove the beef from the oven and leave to rest for 5 minutes at room temperature. Season with salt and pepper on both sides.

7. Serve the beef accompanied by the creamy leeks and cannellini beans.

CHILLI STEAK

with

ROCKET PESTO

Everybody knows traditional basil pesto but it can also be made with other herbs and green leaves. Naturally, I want you to make your own: the flavour of homemade pesto in unbeatable. Here I use peppery rocket and watercress, which work really well with beef, and the kick of chilli in this recipe gives everything an extra boost.

Tagliata di manzo piccante

---

serves 2

1 ciabatta, cut into 2cm chunks
4 tablespoons olive oil
2 x 300g sirloin steaks
1 red chilli, halved, deseeded
and chopped
2 tablespoons extra virgin
olive oil

for the rocket pesto:
75g rocket leaves
1 small garlic clove, peeled
25g pine nuts
125ml extra virgin olive oil
Juice of ½ lemon
50g Parmesan cheese
Salt, to taste

1 Preheat the oven to 200°C/gas 6. Put a large frying pan over a high heat.

2 Tip the ciabatta chunks onto a baking tray and spread out in a single layer. Drizzle with half the olive oil and season with salt. Cook in the oven for 10 minutes.

3 Rub the steaks with the remaining olive oil and cook in the frying pan for 3 minutes on each side.

4 Meanwhile, put the chilli on a large plate, pour over 2 tablespoons of extra virgin olive oil and season with salt.

5 Transfer the steaks to the plate with the chilli, oil and salt. Turn them over in the seasoned oil and cover with foil to keep warm.

6 Put the rocket leaves, garlic and pine nuts in a food processor, add half the extra virgin olive oil and blitz until smooth. Add the remaining oil and lemon juice and grate in the Parmesan cheese. Blitz once more until smooth. Season with a little salt.

7 Thinly slice the steaks and arrange on a large serving plate, drizzle over the rocket pesto and serve immediately, surrounded by the warm croûtons. Serve with my Honey Beetroot (see page 186) if you wish.

STEAK

in

A RED WINE BUTTER SAUCE

It's so easy to make herb butters for fish and steaks. This one takes a little more time but if you double the recipe, roll it into a sausage shape in clingfilm and freeze it, the next time you have a steak or simple chicken breast, you can cut off a slice and melt it in a hot pan for an instant sauce.

Bistecca al vino rosso e burro

serves 4

150g salted butter, softened
1 small onion, peeled and finely chopped
1 teaspoon thyme leaves
1 teaspoon caster sugar
300ml red wine
4 x 175g steaks, cut of your choice
2 tablespoons olive oil
Green salad leaves, to serve
Extra virgin olive oil, to taste
Juice of ½ lemon
Salt and black pepper, to taste

1 Melt 25g butter in a small saucepan and add the onion, thyme leaves and sugar. Season with a pinch of salt and cook for 2 minutes until the onions are translucent.

2 Pour in the wine and gently cook for 8 minutes. Stir occasionally with a wooden spoon.

3 Meanwhile, preheat a large frying pan over a high heat.

4 Rub the steaks with the oil and cook in the hot frying pan for 3 minutes on each side. Transfer to a plate and season with salt and pepper. Cover with foil to keep warm and set aside.

5 Put the remaining butter in a bowl and season with black pepper. Pour the wine sauce over the butter and beat together. (If you want to freeze this sauce for a later date, leave it to cool, roll in clingfilm to form a sausage-shape and pop into the freezer.)

6 Put the steaks in the middle of 4 serving plates and drizzle over the red wine butter sauce.

7 Serve with the salad leaves drizzled with extra virgin olive oil and a squeeze of lemon juice.

FILLET STEAKS

coated

IN BLACK PEPPER AND FRESH ROSEMARY

Fillet steak is the most tender of all the steaks but although it gives great texture it often lacks flavour. I think fillet needs a helping hand so a thick pepper crust works wonders bringing this cut of meat to life.

Filetto di manzo al pepe nero

---

serves 4

4 tablespoons coarse ground black pepper
4 x 175g fillet steaks
4 tablespoons olive oil
2 tablespoons fresh rosemary leaves
50ml brandy
200ml double cream
Salt, to taste

for the rice:
2 teaspoons vegetable stock powder
200g long grain white rice
200g frozen peas, defrosted

1 Measure out 600ml of boiling water from the kettle. Pour into a medium saucepan and add the stock powder and rice.

2 Cover with a lid and bring to the boil. Reduce the heat and gently cook for 10 minutes. Once all the water has been absorbed, stir in the peas, cover with the lid and remove from the heat. Leave the rice to stand.

3 Put the black pepper on a plate and use it to coat the steaks on both sides.

4 Heat the oil in a large frying pan and cook the peppered steaks, with the rosemary leaves, for 3 minutes on each side.

5 Transfer the steaks to a plate and season with salt. Cover with foil to keep warm. Set aside.

6 Pour the brandy into the frying pan and cook for 1 minute. Stir with a wooden spoon and make sure that you scrape all the bits from the bottom of the pan. Pour in the cream, stir together and cook for a further 2 minutes. Season with salt.

7 Simply arrange the rice in the middle of 4 serving plates, top with the steaks and drizzle over the beautiful brandy sauce. Buon Appetito!

BEEF STRIPS

in

PORCINI MUSHROOM SAUCE

Beef and mushrooms are a match made in heaven, whether in a pie or a stew. Fresh porcini mushrooms are really expensive so using a few dried ones given you the depth of flavour without the expense. They are a perfect storecupboard ingredient as they last for months and once soaked in boiling water add a hit of flavour to sauces and even your Sunday roast's gravy.

Stufatino con porcini

serves 4

150g dried porcini mushrooms
300g basmati rice
450g sirloin steak
4 tablespoons olive oil
250g chestnut mushrooms, sliced
1 garlic clove, peeled
1 teaspoon thyme leaves
50ml red wine
3 tablespoons freshly chopped flatleaf parsley
150g mascarpone cheese
Salt and black pepper, to taste

1 Put the porcini mushrooms in a bowl and pour over enough boiling water from the kettle to cover. Set aside for 5 minutes.

2 Pour the rice into a measuring jug and read off how much you have, then tip the rice into a medium saucepan. Now pour 1½ times the amount of water into the saucepan. Season with ½ teaspoon of salt, cover with a lid and put over the heat. Bring to the boil and simmer for 6 minutes or until all the water has completely evaporated. Remove from the heat and leave to stand for 10 minutes with the lid on.

3 Meanwhile, cut the steak into 0.5cm strips. Heat half the oil in a large frying pan and fry the steak for 1 minute on each side just to take on a little colour. Transfer to a plate, cover with foil and set aside.

4 Pour the remaining oil into the frying pan and fry the chestnut mushrooms for 2 minutes. Stir occasionally with a wooden spoon. Grate in the garlic, add the thyme and cook for a further minute. Pour in the wine, stir together and cook for 2 minutes.

5 Meanwhile, drain the porcini mushrooms and reserve the liquid. Stir the liquid into the frying pan. Roughly chop the mushrooms and add to the sauce.

6 Stir in the parsley and mascarpone cheese then add the meat back to the frying pan. Cook gently for 2 minutes.

7 Season with salt and pepper and serve with the rice.

ITALIAN-STYLE COTTAGE PIE

with

CRUSHED POTATOES

Cottage pie normally takes a while to make: first the sauce and then you need to peel, boil and mash the potatoes – well, with this version there's far less work. Using new potatoes means there is no need to peel them as the skins are so thin, and the added bonus is that you get all the nutrients as well. Grating the onions and carrots cuts down the cooking time, so you can be serving up in 20 minutes.

Torta rustica

serves 4

600g baby new potatoes
5 tablespoons olive oil
150g diced pancetta or lardons
**2 tablespoons fresh rosemary
leaves, finely chopped**
**1 medium onion, peeled and
grated**
2 carrots, unpeeled and grated
500g minced beef
1 tablespoon plain flour
1 tablespoon tomato purée
200ml hot beef stock
**50g freshly grated Parmesan
cheese**
Salt and black pepper, to taste

1 Preheat the grill to moderate.

2 Put the potatoes in a large saucepan, cover with boiling water from the kettle, add 1 teaspoon of salt and cook for 10 minutes.

3 Meanwhile, heat 3 tablespoons of the olive oil in a medium saucepan and cook the pancetta and rosemary for 2 minutes over a high heat. Stir occasionally with a wooden spoon.

4 Add the grated onion and carrots to the saucepan and cook for a further 2 minutes.

5 Add the minced beef and use a wooden spoon to break up the meat. Continue to cook for 3 minutes.

6 Stir in the flour and tomato purée and cook for 1 minute. Pour in the stock and continue to cook for 8 minutes. Stir occasionally.

7 Drain the potatoes and return to the same saucepan. Use a potato masher to crush the potatoes. Add the remaining olive oil and Parmesan cheese. Mix together and season with salt and pepper.

8 Spoon the meat sauce into an ovenproof dish and top with the crushed potatoes. Put the dish under the grill for 2 minutes until lightly browned.

9 Enjoy with a bottle of Italian red wine.

FISH & SEAFOOD

Fish and seafood such as mussels, prawns or scallops are the perfect ingredients for dinner if you haven't got much time as they can all be cooked easily within 20 minutes. This chapter features fish fillets or smaller whole fish such as red mullet and sea bream so there's no time wasted in any messy or complicated preparation. The only recipe that is a little bit trickier is the lobster, but it's such an indulgent recipe that it's certainly worth any extra effort and is perfect for celebrations or special occasions when you haven't had much time to prepare.

Pesce e frutti di mare

SCALLOPS

with

PEPPER AND TOMATO SALSA

Every single time I have prepared this dish for guests, they have been really impressed and have often commented that they have never tasted anything quite like it. The juicy scallops (try to buy big ones) are perfect combined with the tomato salsa.

Capesante e peperoni

serves 4

12 scallops, white flesh only
2 tablespoons olive oil
Juice of 1 lemon
50g salted butter
A handful of pea shoots, to serve

for the salsa:
4 tablespoons olive oil
2 garlic cloves, peeled and sliced
1 yellow pepper, cut into
0.5cm dice
4 large ripe plum tomatoes,
deseeded and diced
Salt and black pepper, to taste

1. To make the salsa, heat the olive oil in a large frying pan over a medium heat and fry the garlic for 30 seconds. Add the yellow peppers and cook for 2 minutes before stirring in the tomatoes. Warm them through for a minute before seasoning with salt and pepper. Set aside.

2. Wash the scallops under cold running water and pat dry with kitchen paper. Season with salt and pepper.

3. Add the olive oil to a large frying pan over a high heat and fry the scallops for 1 minute on each side. Squeeze over the lemon juice, remove the scallops from the pan and place on a plate.

4. Add the butter to the pan and season with salt and pepper.

5. To serve, place the salsa in the middle of each serving plate and arrange 3 scallops on top.

6. Drizzle over the lemon butter sauce and scatter with pea shoots. Serve immediately.

MUSSELS AND CLAMS STEW

in a

CREAMY PAPRIKA SAUCE

If I'm eating out, I often order seafood simply cooked with garlic and wine but I have to say I really like the creamy paprika sauce in this recipe (if I do say so myself). It makes the dish really indulgent. For me, the nicest way to serve this stew is in a large pot in the centre of the table and let everyone to dig in. Make sure you have loads of crusty bread for the sauce – you'll be fighting over the last dunk!

Cozze e vongole alla paprika

serves 4

1kg mussels
1kg clams
4 tablespoons olive oil
1 large white onion, peeled and finely sliced
100ml white wine
200ml double cream
4 tablespoons freshly chopped chives
½ teaspoon smoked paprika
Salt, to taste

1   Wash the mussels and clams under cold running water, discarding any broken ones and those that do not close when tapped firmly.

2   Heat the oil in a large saucepan and fry the onion for 3 minutes until soft. Stir with a wooden spoon.

3   Add the mussels and clams and pour over the wine. Stir well, cover the saucepan with a lid and cook over a medium heat for 4 minutes.

4   Remove the lid and pour in the cream with the chives and paprika. Season with salt, stir and continue to cook for a further 3 minutes by which time the sauce will have slightly thickened.

5   Serve the stew immediately, discarding any mussels or clams that have not fully opened.

GRILLED KING PRAWNS

with

ASPARAGUS AND WALNUTS

I wanted to come up with a dish using prawns that could be eaten hot or cold, with more of a salad feel than a main meal. You get all the nutritional benefit from the asparagus and the prawns (both extremely good for you) as they are so lightly cooked and, more importantly, the full flavour. Walnuts add taste and texture – or you could use pine nuts if you prefer.

Gamberoni alla griglia

serves 4

500g asparagus spears, trimmed
12 large raw king prawns, head and shells on
8 tablespoons extra virgin olive oil
1 unwaxed lemon, cut in half
2 tablespoons freshly chopped flatleaf parsley
100g walnuts halves
Salt and pepper, to taste

1 Preheat a griddle pan over a high heat.

2 Fill a medium saucepan with water, bring it to the boil and cook the asparagus for 1 minute. Drain and set aside to cool slightly.

3 Drizzle the asparagus and the prawns with 4 tablespoons of oil. Season with salt and pepper.

4 Cook on the preheated griddle pan for 5 minutes, turning regularly to ensure an even colouring.

5 To make the dressing, pour the remaining oil into a small bowl, squeeze in the juice of half the lemon and add the parsley together with a little salt and pepper. Whisk to combine.

6 Once the asparagus and prawns are ready, arrange on a large serving plate and drizzle over the dressing. Cut the remaining pieces of lemon into 4 wedges and serve around the dish.

7 Finally, scatter over the walnuts and serve.

KING PRAWNS

in

GARLIC AND CHILLI TOMATO SAUCE

Prawns are a big winner in the D'Acampo family and this recipe is one of my favourites. I often prepare this as a starter but also serve it for lunch as it is surprisingly filling. It gives you the kick that you would expect from the spicy sauce and yet is very light in texture. To make a much more substantial meal add cooked pasta to this – amazing!

Gamberoni arrabbiata

serves 4

6 tablespoons olive oil
6 canned anchovy fillets in oil, drained
1 teaspoon dried chilli flakes
2 garlic cloves, peeled and sliced
6 tablespoons pitted green olives in oil or brine, drained
2 tablespoons capers in salt, rinsed under cold water and drained
2 x 400g cans chopped tomatoes
4 tablespoons freshly chopped basil
16 large raw king prawns, head and shells on
Salt, to taste

1 Heat the oil in a large frying pan over a medium heat and cook the anchovies for 3 minutes until they dissolve. Add in the chilli with the garlic and continue to fry for a further minute. Stir occasionally with a wooden spoon.

2 Stir in the olives and capers. Pour in the chopped tomatoes, add the basil and season with salt – but be careful as the anchovies are already salty. Simmer for 8 minutes, uncovered. Stir occasionally.

3 Add the prawns to the sauce and continue to cook for a further 6 minutes. After the first 3 minutes, turn the prawns onto the other side.

4 To serve, divide the sauce equally between each serving plate and place 4 prawns on top. Try to cross 2 prawns together so they can sit up on the plate.

5 Enjoy my spicy prawns with warm crusty bread and a glass of cold Prosecco.

FRESH LOBSTER

with

CHILLI, GARLIC AND EXTRA VIRGIN OLIVE OIL

This recipe is a bit more extravagant, not in terms of preparation but in terms of cost. Any guests will consider themselves very lucky if you decide to make this meal for them. Once in a while this is worth indulging in – even if it's just for yourself… why not?!? There aren't many ingredients here as I want to keep things quick and simple and not take too much attention away from the lobster – that has to be the star of the show.

Aragosta aglio, olio e peperoncino

serves 4

2 large whole live lobsters (approx. 1.5kg each)
Juice of 2 lemons
8 tablespoons extra virgin olive oil
3 garlic cloves, peeled and crushed
½ teaspoon dried chilli flakes
Salt, to taste

1 Fill a very large pot with boiling water from the kettle. Add 1 tablespoon of salt and bring to the boil. Plunge the live lobsters into the boiling water and cook for 10 minutes exactly.

2 Meanwhile, prepare a very large bowl of cold water, adding in a few ice cubes if necessary. Remove the lobsters from the boiling water and drop immediately into the cold water for 3 minutes. Remove and drain.

3 Preheat the grill to the highest setting.

4 Place the lobsters on their backs on a large chopping board and, holding them steady with your free hand, use a large heavy knife to cut from the top of the head straight down to the end of the tail. Turn them over and use the same technique to cut through the shell on the back. By now you should have each lobster separated in two halves.

5 Twist the claws away from the body and use a large knife to cut the shells by holding the knife in place and banging the top of it down with the other hand. Pick out the flesh and place on top of the lobster halves.

6 Squeeze the lemon juice all over the flesh and drizzle over the oil. Spread the crushed garlic over the lobster flesh and sprinkle over the chilli flakes. Season with salt.

7 Place the prepared halves, flesh-side up, under the hot grill for 1 minute. Don't overcook the lobster otherwise it will be chewy. Serve immediately accompanied with a fresh salad of your choice.

SLICED TUNA STEAK

with

PARSLEY, LEMON AND GARLIC DRESSING

Fish is incredibly good for you and tuna is a really top superfood. A meaty tuna steak is a great source of lean protein and packed with nutritious vitamins B12 and D, calcium and iron. The flavour is great and in my opinion tuna shouldn't be smothered with thick rich sauces, which is why I love this recipe: it's light, full of fresh flavour and the fish takes centre stage.

Bistecca di tonno con gremolata

serves 4

4 tuna steaks, each about 150g and 1cm thick
8 tablespoons extra virgin olive oil
50g crisp mixed salad leaves
100g rocket leaves
15 yellow cherry tomatoes, halved
3 tablespoons balsamic vinegar
Salt and black pepper, to taste

for the gremolata:
4 tablespoons flatleaf parsley
2 garlic cloves, peeled
Zest of 1 large unwaxed lemon

1 Preheat a griddle pan over a high heat.

2 To prepare the gremolata dressing, place the parsley and the garlic on a chopping board and finely chop together using a sharp knife. Place in a bowl and grate over the lemon zest. Mix together and set aside.

3 With your fingertips, rub the tuna steaks with 3 tablespoons of oil. Cook on the hot griddle pan for 2 minutes on each side.

4 Place the tuna steaks on a chopping board, season with salt and pepper and leave to rest for 1 minute.

5 Meanwhile, place all the salad leaves and the tomatoes in a large bowl, pour over the remaining oil and the balsamic vinegar. Season with salt and pepper and mix well using your fingertips. Arrange the salad on a serving plate.

6 Using a long sharp knife, cut the tuna on the diagonal into 1cm slices and lay alongside the salad leaves.

7 Sprinkle over the gremolata and serve with a bottle of chilled Italian white wine.

TUNA AND RED ONION SALAD

with

TOASTED GARLIC BREAD

This recipe reminds me of my time fishing with my father and grandfather. We always used to make this dish and take it in huge plastic containers on our little boat when we went out on a trip together: a great memory. This simple salad is brilliantly tasty and refreshing to eat in the heat of summer, yet it really fills you up for the day. We may not have always brought back any fish but we always returned with empty containers!

Insalata di tonno

serves 4

1 x 400g can cannellini beans,
drained and rinsed
1 x 400g can red kidney beans,
drained and rinsed
1 x 400g can butter beans,
drained and rinsed
1 large red onion, peeled and
finely sliced
Juice of ½ unwaxed lemon
6 tablespoons extra virgin
olive oil
3 tablespoons freshly chopped
flatleaf parsley
8 slices of ciabatta, 1cm thick
2 garlic cloves, peeled
3 x 200g cans tuna chunks in
oil, drained
Salt and white pepper, to taste

1   Put all the beans in a large bowl with the sliced onion.

2   Squeeze in the lemon juice and pour over the oil.

3   Add the parsley and season with salt and pepper. Mix together, cover the bowl with a tea towel and set aside for 10 minutes at room temperature. Stir every couple of minutes.

4   Meanwhile, toast the bread and once cool enough to handle, gently rub the garlic on both sides.

5   Gently fold the tuna into the bean salad and serve immediately with the toasted garlic bread.

COD FILLETS
in
A SPICY GARLIC AND TOMATO SAUCE

I love a good simple Arrabbiata sauce and often have it with pasta. This recipe came about when I had extra sauce left over. I decided to top some fish with the remaining sauce and to be honest I was a little bit worried that the chilli in the sauce might overpower the fish but it worked surprisingly well. You'll want some fresh crusty bread to mop up every bit of sauce on your plate.

Merluzzo Arrabbiata

serves 4

4 tablespoons extra virgin olive oil
3 garlic cloves, peeled and quartered
1 large red chilli, deseeded and finely chopped
2 x 400g cans cherry tomatoes
3 tablespoons freshly chopped flatleaf parsley
4 x 200g skinless cod fillets
Salt, to taste

1 Heat the oil in a medium frying pan and fry the garlic and chilli for 30 seconds. Add the cherry tomatoes with the parsley, stir together with a wooden spoon and bring to the boil.

2 Season with salt and gently simmer for 6 minutes, uncovered. Stir occasionally.

3 Carefully slip the cod fillets into the sauce, cover with a lid and cook for 4 minutes on each side. If the sauce is getting too thick, add a couple of tablespoons of hot water.

4 To serve, remove the cod from the pan and place on a large serving plate.

5 Spoon the sauce over the fish and serve hot with your favourite salad on the side.

COD FILLETS
with
SALAMI, CHERRY TOMATOES AND ROSEMARY

Cod is such an excellent fish – firm, meaty and delicious served simply with salt and olive oil or with a sauce; it really is a fish that can go with most things. I like this recipe as the ingredients remind me of my home in Naples. You can substitute the salami with chorizo or pancetta if you prefer.

Merluzzo alla Napoletana

serves 4

500g baby potatoes, skin on
30g salted butter
3 tablespoons olive oil
100g salame Napoli, skin removed, cut into 1cm cubes
4 cod fillets, each about 150g, skin on
100ml white wine
300g cherry tomatoes, halved
1 tablespoon fresh rosemary leaves, finely chopped
Salt and black pepper, to taste

1   Put the potatoes in a large saucepan, cover with boiling water from the kettle, add a teaspoon of salt and boil for 10 minutes. Drain, cut the potatoes in half and set aside.

2   Heat the butter and oil in a large frying pan over a medium heat and fry the salami for 2 minutes. Stir occasionally with a wooden spoon.

3   Add the cod to the frying pan, skin-side down first, and cook for 4 minutes. Gently turn the fillets and cook for a further minute. Lift the fish out of the pan and place onto a warm plate, cover with foil and set aside.

4   Add the wine, tomatoes and rosemary to the pan and let everything bubble away for 2 minutes. Add in the cooked potatoes and continue to cook for a further minute to heat through. Season with salt and pepper.

5   Spoon the potatoes and sauce into the centre of each serving plate and gently place the cod fillets on top. Serve immediately.

ROASTED SEA BREAM

with

LEMON COUSCOUS SALAD

If you like fresh fish that just melts in the mouth, this recipe is for you. It is so tasty with hardly any ingredients added to it. You could also use sea bass or monkfish if you prefer but sea bream definitely has a more delicate flavour, which is beautifully enhanced by the rosemary and garlic.

Orata al forno con couscous

serves 4

4 whole sea bream, about 400g each, scaled and gutted
20 sprigs of fresh rosemary
4 garlic cloves, peeled and halved
4 tablespoons extra virgin olive oil
Salt and black pepper, to taste

for the couscous:
250g couscous
650ml hot vegetable stock
50ml extra virgin olive oil
grated zest and juice of 3 unwaxed lemons
3 tablespoons capers in vinegar, drained
6 tablespoons fresh mint leaves, finely shredded
20 cherry tomatoes, halved

1   Preheat the oven to 200°C/gas 6.

2   Put each fish on a chopping board and with the help of a sharp knife slash each side twice diagonally.

3   Insert 3 rosemary sprigs and 2 garlic halves into the belly cavity of each sea bream: place the remaining rosemary in the slashes. Allow the rosemary to hang out as this will burn, giving an extra flavour to the fish.

4   Put all the fish on a large roasting tray, drizzle with the oil and sprinkle with salt and pepper.

5   Roast in the middle of the oven for 18 minutes until the flesh is white and the skin crispy.

6   Meanwhile, put the couscous into a large bowl and pour over the vegetable stock. Cover tightly with clingfilm and leave it to rest for 5 minutes. Use a fork to fluff up the couscous and separate the grains.

7   Gently fold the remaining ingredients into the cooked couscous and set aside for 5 minutes allowing all the flavours to combine.

8   Serve the lemon couscous with the roasted sea bream.

FILLET OF SALMON

with

SUN-DRIED TOMATO PESTO

I often top fish such as cod and haddock with a green pesto sauce but I wanted to come up with a red pesto fish recipe. I love red pesto and the intense flavour of the sun-dried tomatoes and the kick of the chilli are really potent here. The salmon works so well with these flavours and the dish looks amazing with its pink/red bright colours against a serving of plain white rice. A good glass of Italian red completes the theme.

Salmone al pesto rosso

serves 4

4 salmon fillets, each about 200g, skin on or off

for the pesto:
1 x 400g can chopped tomatoes
1 garlic clove, peeled
8 basil leaves
50g capers in brine, drained
1 teaspoon dried chilli flakes
200g sun-dried tomatoes in oil, drained
1 tablespoon extra virgin olive oil
Salt, to taste

1   Preheat the oven to 190°C/gas 5.

2   Put the tomatoes, garlic, basil, capers, chilli flakes and sun-dried tomatoes in a food processor, drizzle over the extra virgin olive oil and blitz until you have a smooth creamy paste. Season with a little salt.

3   Put the salmon fillets on a baking tray and spoon the spicy paste over each one. (Place them skin-side down if the salmon comes with the skin on.)

4   Cook in the hot oven for 15 minutes.

5   Remove the tray from the oven and leave the salmon to rest for 1 minute.

6   Serve hot with simple boiled rice to accompany the fish and a big glass of Italian red wine.

SALMON
and
SPINACH FISHCAKES

Many people buy ready-made fishcakes, perhaps because they feel it's going to be a long difficult process to make them. Well, it couldn't be easier: you put most of the ingredients in a food processor, coat the mixture in cracker crumbs and cook – done. I guarantee they will taste better, you will get much more fish than in any ready-made ones, and they probably cost less. Try this recipe – you will never go back!

Tortine di salmone

serves 4

150g frozen leaf spinach, defrosted
16 cream crackers
2 x 180g can salmon chunks in brine, drained
Zest of 1 unwaxed lemon
1 large egg, separated
2 tablespoons freshly chopped flatleaf parsley
4 tablespoons olive oil
3 tablespoons mayonnaise
2 tablespoons wholegrain mustard
Salt and black pepper, to taste

1 Squeeze any excess water from the spinach, roughly chop and set aside.

2 Place 6 crackers in a food processor and blitz to make fine crumbs then tip on to a flat plate and set aside for coating the fishcakes later.

3 Put the remaining crackers in the food processor and blitz until fine. Add in the salmon, spinach, lemon zest, egg yolk, parsley and season with salt and pepper. Blitz until fully combined. Set aside.

4 Put the egg white in a bowl and whisk with a fork.

5 Shape the salmon mixture into 4 patties, dip each one into the egg white and then coat in the reserved cracker crumbs.

6 Heat the oil in a medium frying pan over a medium heat and cook the fishcakes for 5 minutes on each side, until beautiful and golden all over.

7 Meanwhile, put the mayonnaise and mustard in a small bowl and stir.

8 Serve the salmon fishcakes hot with the mustard and mayonnaise dip.

PASTA

La pasta

Pasta is often the dish that people turn to for a quick midweek meal when they're tired and hungry and the cupboards are almost bare. So here are a few ideas to pep up your usual pasta dinners using a range of pasta from fettuccine, spaghetti and linguine to farfalle, rigatoni and penne. If you want to speed up the recipes even more you can always substitute dried pasta with fresh egg pasta, which will roughly halve your cooking time.

BAKED RED MULLET

with

OREGANO, CHERRY TOMATOES AND WHITE WINE

Considering how simple this recipe is to prepare, the 'Ooohhs!' I get when I serve it up always amaze me. I don't know whether it's the smell of the fish and wine or the way you have to peel open your own foil parcel to reveal your meal, but whatever it is, everyone seems to love it. You can serve this with a crisp salad or with couscous, rice or potatoes.

Triglie al forno

serves 4

4 whole red mullet, each about 250g, scaled and gutted
1 small bunch of fresh oregano
4 garlic cloves, peeled and halved
100ml extra virgin olive oil, plus extra for brushing
100ml dry white wine
Juice of 3 lemons
16 cherry tomatoes, halved
Sea salt and black pepper, to taste

1   Preheat the oven to 220°C/gas 7.

2   Season the fish with salt and pepper inside and out. Put 3 sprigs of oregano and 2 pieces of garlic in the cavity of each one.

3   Prepare four 30cm squares of foil. Brush with a little oil on each square and lay a fish diagonally across the centre of each piece. Bring the sides of the foil up around the fish and crimp together tightly at each end, leaving the top part open.

4   Pour 2 tablespoons of wine into each parcel with 2 tablespoons of lemon juice and 2 tablespoons of extra virgin olive oil.

5   Scatter the cherry tomatoes equally over the top of the mullet.

6   Seal the parcels well and transfer to a baking tray. Bake in the middle of the oven for 10 minutes.

7   To serve, place the unopened parcels on 4 warm serving plates and take them to the table with a large bowl of crisp salad leaves.

8   Enjoy with a cold glass of dry white wine.

GRILLED FILLETS OF MACKEREL

with

OLIVES AND CHERRY TOMATOES

Sgombro con olive e pomodorini

Mackerel is an 'oily fish' and not really eaten as much as it used to be. Many of the older generation still love to use this fish but I think we are losing that tradition, which is a real shame. If you tend only to buy mackerel in its canned form, in oil or tomato sauce, this recipe using fresh fillets will make you think again – it's an absolute treat cooked Italian-style: marinated first, then cooked super-fast on a hot griddle. Historically in England, this fish was not preserved, but was consumed only in its fresh form but now with proper refrigeration we can enjoy this fish more often and so I have created this recipe for those of you who love fish and want to try something a little different.

serves 4

5 tablespoons extra virgin olive oil
Juice of 1 large lemon
½ teaspoon smoked paprika
4 whole fresh mackerel, each about 350g, filleted to give 8 pieces in total
60g rocket leaves
100g yellow cherry tomatoes, halved
100g red cherry tomatoes, halved
100g pitted green olives in brine, drained and halved
2 tablespoons balsamic vinegar
Salt, to taste

1   Pour the oil into a medium bowl with the lemon juice. Season with the paprika and ½ teaspoon of salt and mix together.

2   Brush some of the marinade on both sides of the mackerel fillets and leave to marinate on a flat plate for 10 minutes at room temperature.

3   Meanwhile, preheat a griddle pan to high and preheat a medium frying pan.

4   Arrange the rocket leaves in the middle of 4 serving plates.

5   Cook the fillets of mackerel on the hot griddle pan, skin-side down first, for 30 seconds. Turn the fillets and cook the other side for a further 30 seconds.

6   Arrange the mackerel, cherry tomatoes and olives on and around the rocket leaves, trying not flatten the leaves too much.

7   Pour the remaining marinade into the hot frying pan and cook for 30 seconds, stirring continuously with a wooden spoon.

8   Spoon the hot dressing all over the salad and fish and finally drizzle over the balsamic vinegar.

9   Serve hot with crusty bread on the side.

SHELL PASTA

with

PEPPERS, SUN-DRIED TOMATOES AND PINE NUTS

This has to be the ultimate vegetarian pasta recipe. There is so much goodness in this dish and it's also really filling and extremely tasty. Some might think that the peppers could make it slightly bitter but together with the pine nuts and basil, it screams freshness and will be enjoyed by herbivores and carnivores alike.

Conchiglie vegetariane

serves 4

1 orange pepper
1 red pepper
8 tablespoons olive oil
2 garlic cloves, peeled and finely sliced
8–10 sun-dried tomatoes, sliced
25g pine nuts
500g medium conchiglie shells
Basil leaves, to garnish
Salt and black pepper, to taste

1 In a large saucepan, bring 5 litres of water to the boil with 1½ tablespoons of fine salt.

2 On a chopping board, with the help of a sharp knife, cut the peppers in half, discard the seeds and chop into 1cm cubes.

3 Heat the olive oil in a large frying pan over a medium heat and fry the garlic and peppers for 5 minutes. Stir occasionally with a wooden spoon. Season with salt and pepper before adding in the sun-dried tomatoes and pine nuts. Cook for 2 minutes.

4 Meanwhile, cook the pasta in the boiling water until al dente. To get the al dente perfect bite, cook the pasta for 1 minute less then instructed on the packet and always leave the pan uncovered. A good-quality dried pasta will take 8–10 minutes to cook.

5 Once the pasta is cooked, drain and tip it back into the same saucepan that you cooked it in.

6 Pour over the prepared sauce, put the saucepan over a medium heat and mix all of the ingredients together for 30 seconds allowing all the flavours to combine beautifully. Scatter with basil leaves then divide the pasta between 4 serving plates and serve immediately.

FETTUCCINE

with

GOAT'S CHEESE, CHERRY TOMATOES AND FRESH BASIL

Goat's cheese is a favourite in our house but it can be quite heavy when melted, so using it in a pasta recipe can sometimes not work, unless it's a baked pasta dish. However, I came up with the perfect solution – don't melt it completely. My family love the strong yet fresh flavour of this recipe and actually getting protein, calcium, vitamins and carbs in one dish is not bad going. If you're a fan of goat's cheese you too will love this, but it also works well with feta if you prefer a slightly milder flavour.

Fettuccine velocissime

serves 4

8 tablespoons extra virgin olive oil
2 garlic cloves, peeled and finely sliced
300g cherry tomatoes, halved
500g fresh egg fettuccine
10 basil leaves, finely sliced, plus extra to garnish
150g firm goat's cheese
Salt and white pepper, to taste

1   Bring 5 litres of water to the boil in a large saucepan with 1½ tablespoons of fine salt.

2   In a medium frying pan, add the oil and gently fry the garlic and cherry tomatoes for 2 minutes, stirring with a wooden spoon. Season with salt and pepper then remove from the heat and set aside.

3   Meanwhile, cook the pasta in the boiling water until al dente. To get the al dente perfect bite, cook the pasta for 1 minute less than instructed on the packet and always keep the pan uncovered. A good-quality fresh egg pasta will take 4–6 minutes to cook.

4   Once the pasta is cooked, drain and tip back into the same saucepan in which you cooked it.

5   Pour over the cherry tomato mixture, add the basil and crumble in the goat's cheese. Gently fold together, away from the heat, for 30 seconds allowing all the flavours to combine.

6   Serve immediately, garnished with fresh basil leaved and accompanied with a glass of your favourite cold beer.

PASTA

with

CRISPY FOUR CHEESE SAUCE TOPPING

You will often find this recipe in Italian cookery books and I did think twice about putting it in this book but it would be so wrong to leave out such a wonderful classic. I always make this dish with the four wonderful Italian cheeses below but, to be honest, most cheeses will work. What's great about this particular dish is that if you don't have time to prepare it when your friends/family/guests arrive, you also have the option of preparing it in the morning and simply baking it when needed.

Penne ai quattro formaggi

serves 4

250ml full-fat milk
100g Gorgonzola, cut into cubes
100g Taleggio, cut into cubes
1 teaspoon smoked paprika
500g penne rigate
1 x 125g mozzarella ball, drained and cut into cubes
100g freshly grated Parmesan cheese
Salt, to taste

1 Bring 5 litres of water to the boil in a large saucepan with 1½ tablespoons of fine salt.

2 Pour the milk into a medium saucepan over a medium heat and add the Gorgonzola and Taleggio cheese. Gently melt the cheeses in the milk for 5 minutes, stirring with a wooden spoon.

3 Once the cheeses are melted, stir in the smoked paprika and season with a little salt. Set aside.

4 Preheat the grill to its highest setting (if you intend to serve the dish straight away).

5 Meanwhile, cook the pasta in the boiling water until al dente. To get the al dente perfect bite, cook the pasta for 1 minute less than instructed on the packet and always keep the pan uncovered. A good-quality driespasta will take 8–10 minutes to cook.

6 Once the pasta is cooked, drain and tip back into the same saucepan in which you cooked it.

7 Pour over the cheese sauce, add the cubes of mozzarella and half of the grated Parmesan and stir together for 10 seconds allowing the sauce to coat the pasta perfectly. Tip the pasta into an ovenproof dish and sprinkle over the remaining Parmesan cheese. Put under the hot grill for 3 minutes until golden and crispy.

FETTUCCINE

in

A CLASSIC BASIL AND TOMATO SAUCE

I know you might think this is quite a basic recipe but I am a true believer in 'less is more'. The small number of ingredients speak for themselves and I've never met anyone who doesn't like this dish, especially if you have a house full of kids. Do use fresh pasta for this recipe, although you could make it with the ribbon pasta tagliatelle if you prefer.

Fettuccine pomodoro e basilico

serves 4

1 medium white onion, peeled and finely chopped
6 tablespoons extra virgin olive oil
2 x 400g cans chopped tomatoes
10 basil leaves
500g fresh egg fettuccine
Salt and black pepper, to taste
Crusty bread, to serve

1 Bring 5 litres of water to the boil in a large saucepan with 1½ tablespoons of fine salt.

2 Place a medium saucepan over a low heat and fry the onion in the oil for 5 minutes until golden, stirring occasionally with a wooden spoon.

3 Pour in the chopped tomatoes, add the basil, and season with salt and pepper. Continue to cook for 10 minutes, uncovered, stirring the sauce every couple of minutes.

4 Cook the pasta in the boiling water until al dente. To get the al dente perfect bite, cook the pasta for 1 minute less than instructed on the packet and always keep the pan uncovered. A good-quality fresh egg pasta will take 4–6 minutes to cook.

5 Once the pasta is cooked, drain and tip back into the same saucepan in which you cooked it.

6 Pour over the tomato and basil sauce and stir together for 30 seconds allowing the sauce to coat the pasta perfectly.

7 Serve immediately with plenty of warm crusty bread on the side to mop up the delicious tomato sauce.

BOW PASTA

with

RICOTTA AND SUN-DRIED TOMATOES

If you enjoy creamy sauces but don't actually like cream (there are hundreds out there who have this problem), this recipe is for you. Ricotta cheese is an amazing substitute; light, creamy, but without the fat. The sun-dried tomatoes add the essential flavour to what could otherwise be a bland dish; it makes my mouth water just thinking about it.

Farfalle e ricotta

serves 4

**4 tablespoons pine nuts
250g ricotta cheese
150g sun-dried tomatoes in oil, drained and cut into thin strips
5 tablespoons freshly chopped flatleaf parsley
½ teaspoon freshly ground black pepper
4 tablespoons extra virgin olive oil
500g farfalle
Salt, to taste**

1 Bring 5 litres of water to the boil in a large saucepan with 1½ tablespoons of fine salt.

2 In a medium frying pan, toast the pine nuts for 2 minutes until golden brown all over. Watch carefully as they burn easily. Set aside.

3 Put the ricotta in a large bowl with the sun-dried tomatoes, parsley, pine nuts and black pepper. Pour over the oil, add 4 tablespoons hot water and season with salt. Mix together and leave to rest at room temperature.

4 Meanwhile, cook the pasta in the boiling water until al dente. To get the al dente perfect bite, cook the pasta for 1 minute less than instructed on the packet and always keep the pan uncovered. A good-quality driedpasta will take 8–10 minutes to cook.

5 Once the pasta is cooked, drain and tip back into the same saucepan in which you cooked it.

6 Pour over the ricotta mixture and gently fold together for 30 seconds allowing the sauce to coat the pasta perfectly.

7 Serve immediately.

POTATO DUMPLINGS

in

SPICY TOMATO SAUCE WITH MOZZARELLA

The ingredients in this sauce are similar to those you would find on a Margherita pizza, but with the addition of onion and chilli. This is pure comfort food – you feel completely satisfied, content and relaxed after a plate of *gnocchi piccanti alla Napoletana*. Gnocchi is a great substitute for pasta and kids love the little potato dumplings.

Gnocchi piccanti alla Napoletana

serves 4

4 tablespoons extra virgin olive oil
1 medium white onion, peeled and finely chopped
1 teaspoon dried chilli flakes
1 x 700ml bottle of passata
10 fresh basil leaves, plus extra to garnish
500g ready-made plain gnocchi (at least 70 per cent potatoes)
2 x 125g mozzarella balls, drained and cut into 1cm cubes
Salt, to taste

1 Bring 5 litres of water to the boil in a large saucepan with 1½ tablespoons of fine salt.

2 Heat the oil in a medium saucepan over a medium heat and fry the onion and chilli for 3 minutes until golden.

3 Pour in the passata and continue to cook for a further 10 minutes, uncovered. Stir occasionally with a wooden spoon.

4 Stir in the basil, season with salt and remove from the heat.

5 Cook the gnocchi in the boiling salted water until they start to float to the surface. (A good-quality gnocchi will take 3–5 minutes to cook). Drain well and add to the saucepan with the cooked tomato sauce.

6 Return the saucepan to a low heat and cook for 1 minute. Stir occasionally allowing the sauce to coat the potato dumplings.

7 Scatter over the mozzarella and continue to cook, stirring continuously, for a further 30 seconds allowing the mozzarella to melt slightly.

8 Serve immediately, garnished with fresh basil.

SPAGHETTI

with

GARLIC, OLIVE OIL, CHILLI AND CAPERS

If you are on a first date or are hoping to continue your evening maybe this isn't the recipe for you. You risk slurping your spaghetti, dribbling oil on your clothes and reeking of garlic but for any other occasion, this recipe is always a winner. I love the combination of simple yet strong flavours.

Spaghetti aglio, olio, peperoncino e capperi

serves 4

8 tablespoons extra virgin olive oil
4 garlic cloves, peeled and finely sliced
2 medium hot red chillies, deseeded and finely chopped
3 tablespoons salted capers, rinsed under cold water and drained
4 tablespoons freshly chopped flatleaf parsley
500g spaghetti or linguine
Salt, to taste

1   Bring 5 litres of water to the boil in a large saucepan with 1½ tablespoons of fine salt.

2   Heat the oil in a small frying pan over a low heat and fry the garlic for 1 minute until golden, stirring with a wooden spoon. Add the chillies, capers and parsley and fry for a further minute.

3   Pour over 6 tablespoons of the salted water from the saucepan in which you will cook the pasta. Mix and set aside.

4   Meanwhile, cook the pasta in the boiling water until al dente. To get the al dente perfect bite, cook the pasta for 1 minute less than instructed on the packet and always keep the pan uncovered. A good-quality dried pasta will take 8–10 minutes to cook.

5   Once the pasta is cooked, drain and tip back into the same saucepan in which you cooked it.

6   Pour over the chilli and garlic mixture and, over a medium heat, stir together for 15 seconds allowing the flavours to combine beautifully.

7   Serve immediately with a glass of cold Italian dry white wine.

RIGATONI

in

A CREAMY SAFFRON SAUCE

Most people love traditional creamy sauces but I wanted to create one with a bit of a difference, with a special flavour that we don't use very often: saffron. Saffron has a distinctive hay-like fragrance and has a really long medicinal history of healing, some people claim it is cancer-suppressing and even the petals can be helpful for depression. Iran now accounts for some 90 per cent of the world production of saffron; I personally love its unique flavour and extraordinary deep-yellow colour. It's a very expensive ingredient but happily a few threads are all that you need.

Rigatoni allo zafferano

serves 4

2 pinches of saffron threads
40g salted butter
150g Neapolitan salami, roughly chopped
250ml double cream
100g frozen peas, defrosted
500g rigatoni
3 egg yolks
60g freshly grated Pecorino cheese
Salt and black pepper, to taste

1 Bring 5 litres of water to the boil in a large saucepan with 1½ tablespoons of fine salt.

2 Put the saffron in a small bowl with 4 tablespoons of hot water. Set aside to infuse for 5 minutes.

3 Melt the butter in a medium saucepan and gently fry the salami for 2 minutes, stirring occasionally with a wooden spoon.

4 Pour over the cream and the saffron water. Add the peas and gently simmer for 5 minutes. Season with salt and pepper and set aside.

5 Meanwhile, cook the pasta in the boiling water until al dente. To get the al dente perfect bite, cook the pasta for 1 minute less than instructed on the packet and always keep the pan uncovered. A good-quality dried pasta will take 8–10 minutes to cook.

6 Once the pasta is cooked, drain and tip back into the same saucepan in which you cooked it. Pour over the saffron sauce.

7 Put the pan over a low heat and add the egg yolks, stirring continuously for 15 seconds.

8 Serve immediately with grated Pecorino on top.

RIGATONI

with

CHICKEN, RED CHILLIES, GARLIC AND TOMATOES

I once overheard a friend tell her family that she needed to cook chicken because it was almost past its use-by date that night and they were all disappointed as they fancied pasta… hello, Gino to the rescue… I even surprised myself with this one to be honest, as I pretty much threw the ingredients together, but it works. The dish is now on their weekly supper menu at home and it's called 'Gino's night' – I'm very honoured.

Rigatoni con pollo Arrabbiata

serves 4

8 tablespoons extra virgin olive oil
2 medium skinless, boneless chicken breasts, cut into 2cm pieces
2 garlic cloves, peeled and finely sliced
2 medium-hot red chillies, deseeded and finely chopped
2 x 400g cans chopped tomatoes
500g rigatoni
Salt, to taste
Parmesan shavings, to serve (optional)

1   Bring 5 litres of water to the boil in a large saucepan with 1½ tablespoons of fine salt.

2   Heat the oil in a large frying pan over a medium heat and fry the chicken, garlic and chilli for 2 minutes. Stir with a wooden spoon.

3   Pour in the chopped tomatoes, stir well and gently simmer for 10 minutes, uncovered, stirring every couple of minutes. Season with salt once the sauce is ready.

4   Meanwhile, cook the pasta in the boiling water until al dente. To get the al dente perfect bite, cook the pasta for 1 minute less than instructed on the packet and always keep the pan uncovered. A good-quality dried pasta will take 8–10 minutes to cook.

5   Once the pasta is cooked, drain and tip back into the same saucepan in which you cooked it.

6   Pour over the chicken sauce and stir together for 30 seconds allowing the flavours to combine properly.

7   Serve immediately with Parmesan shavings scattered over the top if you wish.

PENNE

with

PANCETTA, ONIONS AND CHOPPED TOMATOES

I cook this recipe at least once a week at home. It is so simple to make, so full of flavour and never fails to remind me of Italy. My late father Ciro loved this pasta dish. Whenever I made it he would ask whether I had used good-quality canned tomatoes, as he didn't like to have skin on them – you would think he wouldn't need to ask, considering he worked for me importing perfect canned tomatoes, but the question would always come and I would always reply, 'Of course, papa'. I think of him every time I make this dish and now miss him asking me.

Penne Amatriciana

serves 4

6 tablespoons olive oil
2 large white onions, peeled and finely sliced
½ teaspoon dried chilli flakes
250g diced pancetta
2 x 400g cans chopped tomatoes
500g penne rigate
4 tablespoons freshly chopped flatleaf parsley
Salt, to taste

1   Bring 5 litres of water to the boil in a large saucepan with 1½ tablespoons of fine salt.

2   Heat the oil in a medium saucepan over a medium heat and fry the onions for 3 minutes, stirring occasionally with a wooden spoon. Add the chilli and pancetta and continue to cook for a further 5 minutes.

3   Pour in the chopped tomatoes, stir well and gently simmer for 10 minutes, uncovered, stirring every couple of minutes. Season with salt once the sauce is cooked.

4   Meanwhile, cook the pasta in the boiling water until al dente. To get the al dente perfect bite, cook the pasta for 1 minute less than instructed on the packet and always keep the pan uncovered. A good-quality dried pasta will take 8–10 minutes to cook.

5   Once the pasta is cooked, drain and tip back into the same saucepan in which you cooked it.

6   Pour over the sauce, add the parsley and stir together for 30 seconds allowing the flavours to combine.

7   Serve immediately with a large glass of Italian red wine.

BOW PASTA

with

EGGS, CRISPY PANCETTA AND PECORINO

Before you go out and buy cream, bacon and mushrooms, please read the ingredients for this recipe. It is a real traditional Italian Carbonara and the ingredients may surprise you. In Italy we make this pasta dish with eggs not cream, and the flavour is far superior. If you prefer you can use Parmesan cheese instead of Pecorino and if making for your kids, omit the parsley.

Farfalle Carbonara

serves 4

3 tablespoons extra virgin olive oil
3 tablespoons salted butter
250g diced pancetta
4 large eggs
6 tablespoons freshly grated Pecorino Romano
4 tablespoons freshly chopped flatleaf parsley
½ teaspoon freshly ground black pepper
500g farfalle
Salt, to taste

1   Bring 5 litres of water to the boil in a large saucepan with 1½ tablespoons of fine salt.

2   Heat the oil and butter in a medium frying pan over a medium heat and fry the pancetta for 5 minutes until golden and crispy, stirring occasionally. Remove from the heat and set aside.

3   Whisk the eggs in a bowl with half the Pecorino cheese, the parsley and black pepper. Season with salt.

4   Meanwhile, cook the pasta in the boiling water until al dente. To get the al dente perfect bite, cook the pasta for 1 minute less than instructed on the packet and always keep the pan uncovered. A good-quality dried pasta will take 8–10 minutes to cook.

5   Once the pasta is cooked, drain and tip back into the same saucepan in which you cooked it.

6   Add the fried pancetta to the pasta and pour over the egg mixture. Mix together for 30 seconds with a wooden spoon. (The heat from the pasta cooks the egg sufficiently to create a creamy and moist texture.) Check if it needs a little more salt and serve immediately with the remaining cheese sprinkled on top.

BOW PASTA

with

TRADITIONAL CREAMY SAUCE, MUSHROOMS AND HAM

When I first came to England, I ordered a Carbonara and got spaghetti with ham, cream and mushrooms. I was surprised as this wasn't Carbonara that a native Italian would recognise but, at the same time, I did like the flavour. I felt it was missing something, though, and came up with this recipe, which I think is a fantastic mixture of the versions of Carbonara made in England and Italy. It makes the dish more interesting, in my opinion, and it's certainly a big success with customers at My Pasta Bar in London.

Farfalle Boscaiola

serves 4

6 tablespoons olive oil
1 large white onion, finely sliced
250g diced cooked ham
100g frozen peas, defrosted
200g chestnut mushrooms, sliced
2 x 400g cans chopped tomatoes
150g mascarpone cheese
500g farfalle
3 tablespoons freshly chopped basil
60g freshly grated Parmesan cheese
Salt and black pepper, to taste

1 Bring 5 litres of water to the boil in a large saucepan with 1½ tablespoons of fine salt.

2 Heat the oil in a large frying pan and fry the onion for 3 minutes over a medium heat, stirring occasionally with a wooden spoon. Add the ham, peas and mushrooms and continue to cook for a further 5 minutes.

3 Pour in the chopped tomatoes, stir well and gently simmer for 8 minutes, uncovered, stirring every couple of minutes. Add the mascarpone and season with salt and pepper. Mix together, remove from the heat and set aside.

4 Meanwhile, cook the pasta in the boiling water until al dente. To get the al dente perfect bite, cook the pasta for 1 minute less than instructed on the packet and always keep the pan uncovered. A good-quality dried pasta will take 8–10 minutes to cook.

5 Once the pasta is cooked, drain and tip back into the same saucepan in which you cooked it.

6 Pour over the sauce and add the basil; stir together for 30 seconds allowing the sauce to coat the pasta perfectly.

7 Serve immediately with the Parmesan cheese sprinkled on top.

BOW PASTA

with

BASIL PESTO AND PRAWNS

This recipe was created during an argument between my boys: Rocco wanted pasta with garlic, prawns and rocket leaves and Luci wanted pesto. Here we are – basil pesto with prawns. It really works; we all absolutely loved it and I got to please both boys without turning my kitchen into a restaurant! Please make sure you only buy fresh basil to make the pesto as the flavour is so much better.

Farfalle al pesto Genovese e gamberi

serves 4

60g basil leaves
50g pine nuts
1 garlic clove, peeled
130ml extra virgin olive oil
30g freshly grated Parmesan cheese
150g cooked peeled large prawns
500g farfalle
Salt and black pepper, to taste

1 Bring 5 litres of water to the boil in a large saucepan with 1½ tablespoons of fine salt.

2 Put the basil, pine nuts and garlic in a food processor. Drizzle in the oil and blitz until smooth.

3 Transfer the basil mixture to a large serving bowl and fold in the Parmesan. Season with salt and pepper and fold in the prawns. Set aside.

4 Meanwhile, cook the pasta in the boiling water until al dente. To get the al dente perfect bite, cook the pasta for 1 minute less than instructed on the packet and always keep the pan uncovered. A good-quality dried pasta will take 8–10 minutes to cook.

5 Just before the pasta is ready to be drained, remove 4 tablespoons of the boiling water from the pan and add to the bowl with the pesto mixture.

6 Once the pasta is cooked, drain and tip it into the bowl with the pesto mixture.

7 Fold together for 30 seconds allowing the pesto to coat the pasta.

8 Serve immediately.

FETTUCCINE

with

ANCHOVIES, TOMATOES, GARLIC AND CAPERS

Anchovies are like Marmite – you either love them or hate them. If you are a lover like me, you have to try this recipe. It is a really strong, rich flavoured pasta dish. I love this sauce so much I've even used it to marinate cod and chicken fillets – it's great on nearly everything and the best part is dunking bread in any leftover sauce.

Fettuccine con acciughe

serves 4

8 tablespoons olive oil
2 garlic cloves, peeled and finely sliced
12 anchovy fillets in oil, drained and chopped
½ teaspoon dried chilli flakes
50g capers in salt, rinsed under cold water and drained
100g good-quality pitted green olives, halved
2 x 400g cans chopped tomatoes
500g fresh egg fettuccine
3 tablespoons freshly chopped flatleaf parsley
Salt, to taste
Crusty bread, to serve

1 Bring 5 litres of water to the boil in a large saucepan with 1½ tablespoons of fine salt.

2 Heat the oil in a large frying pan over a medium heat and fry the garlic and anchovies for about 2 minutes, stirring occasionally with a wooden spoon.

3 Add in the chilli, capers and olives and continue to cook for a further 2 minutes. Continue to stir.

4 Pour in the tomatoes, stir well and gently simmer for 10 minutes, uncovered, stirring every couple of minutes. Once ready, season with salt if necessary, remove from the heat and set aside.

5 Meanwhile, cook the pasta in the boiling water until al dente. To get the al dente perfect bite, cook the pasta for 1 minute less than instructed on the packet and always keep the pan uncovered. A good-quality fresh egg pasta will take 4–6 minutes to cook.

6 Once the pasta is cooked, drain and tip back into the same saucepan in which you cooked it.

7 Pour over the anchovy sauce, add the parsley and stir together for 30 seconds, allowing the flavours to combine properly.

8 Serve immediately with a cold Italian beer. Don't forget some bread for mopping up the sauce.

LINGUINE

in

A TUNA AND SMOKED SALMON SAUCE

This is a very tasty yet light pasta dish, which is incredibly easy to prepare. Seafood can be expensive, though, so I created a recipe that will give you your fish fix and yet won't make you feel as if you're being extravagant. As smoked salmon is expensive; I've increased the fish factor here by using a can of tuna as well. Please make sure you use tuna in oil and not brine – the flavour is so much better.

Linguine al tonno e salmone

serves 4

10 tablespoons extra virgin olive oil
2 garlic cloves, peeled and finely sliced
100g Kalamata pitted olives, drained and halved
150g smoked salmon, cut into strips
10 cherry tomatoes, quartered
½ teaspoon dried chilli flakes
1 x 200g can tuna chunks in oil, drained
2 tablespoons freshly chopped flatleaf parsley
500g linguine
Salt, to taste

1 Bring 5 litres of water to the boil in a large saucepan with 1½ tablespoons of fine salt.

2 Heat the oil in a large frying pan over a medium heat and fry the garlic, olives and smoked salmon for 1 minute. Stir with a wooden spoon.

3 Add in the tomatoes along with the chilli and continue to cook for a further 3 minutes. Stir occasionally.

4 Scatter over the tuna chunks and the parsley, season with a little salt and mix together for a further minute. Remove from the heat and set aside.

5 Meanwhile, cook the pasta in the boiling water until al dente. To get the al dente perfect bite, cook the pasta for 1 minute less than instructed on the packet and always keep the pan uncovered. A good-quality dried pasta will take 8–10 minutes to cook.

7 Once the pasta is cooked, drain and tip back into the same saucepan in which you cooked it.

8 Pour over the tuna and salmon sauce and, over a low heat, stir together for 30 seconds allowing the flavours to combine beautifully.

9 Serve immediately and please, please, DO NOT grate any kind of cheese on top.

SPAGHETTI

with

CRAB, CHERRY TOMATOES AND FRESH RED CHILLIES

If you are having guests over but don't have much time to prepare a meal, this is the recipe for you. Crab is a real treat and makes the dish seem really extravagant. The ingredients are simple and uncomplicated allowing the crabmeat to shine. You could also use lobster if you prefer – I guess it would depend on your budget and how much you like your guests!

Spaghetti con granchio e peperoncino

serves 4

500g spaghetti
8 tablespoons extra virgin olive oil
2 garlic cloves, peeled and finely sliced
1 medium hot red chilli, deseeded and finely sliced
200g cherry tomatoes, halved
100ml white wine
200g white crabmeat
3 tablespoons freshly chopped chives
Salt, to taste

1 In a large saucepan, bring 5 litres of water to the boil with 1½ tablespoons of fine salt.

2 Cook the pasta in the boiling water until al dente. To get the al dente perfect bite, cook the pasta for 1 minute less then instructed on the packet and always leave the pan uncovered. A good-quality dried pasta will take 8–10 minutes to cook.

3 Meanwhile, gently heat the oil in a large frying pan and fry the garlic and chilli together for 30 seconds.

4 Add the tomatoes and cook for 2 minutes before deglazing the pan with the wine. Bring to a simmer before stirring in the crab. Cook for 1 minute to warm the crab through.

5 Once the pasta is cooked, drain well before tipping into the pan with the crab sauce. Stir to combine, sprinkle over the chopped chives and serve immediately.

LINGUINE

---
with

CLAMS AND WHITE WINE

I absolutely love this recipe, so much so I would say it's my favourite in this chapter. I lived on freshly landed seafood when I was a young boy and miss it hugely. This was, and still is, number one for me. It's so easy and yet you really feel that you have been spoiled when someone makes it for you. Please be careful when making the sauce and ensure that you do not stir the clams too vigorously or you run the risk of breaking bits of the shell into the sauce.

Linguine vongole e vino bianco
---

serves 4

700g fresh clams in their shells
50ml dry white wine
8 tablespoons extra virgin olive oil
3 garlic cloves, peeled and sliced
½ teaspoon dried chilli flakes
15 cherry tomatoes, halved
4 tablespoons freshly chopped flatleaf parsley
500g linguine
Salt, to taste

1　Bring 5 litres of water to the boil in a large saucepan with 1½ tablespoons of fine salt.

2　Wash the clams under cold running water, discarding any broken ones and any that do not close when tapped firmly.

3　Put a large saucepan over a high heat, carefully add the clams and pour over the wine. Cover with a lid and cook for 3 minutes until they have opened. Discard any that remain closed. Tip into a colander placed over a large bowl and set aside, reserving the cooking liquor.

4　Pour the oil into the same saucepan in which you cooked the clams and gently fry the garlic for 1 minute until it begins to sizzle. Add the chilli, tomatoes and parsley and pour in the reserved liquor from the clams. Cook over a medium heat for 5 minutes. Season with salt.

5　Meanwhile, cook the pasta in the boiling water until al dente. To get the al dente perfect bite, cook the pasta for 1 minute less than instructed on the packet and always keep the pan uncovered. A good-quality dried pasta will take 8–10 minutes to cook.

6　Once the pasta is cooked, drain and tip back into the same saucepan in which you cooked it.

7　Pour over the sauce, add the clams and very gently stir together over a low heat for 30 seconds allowing the sauce to thicken and coat the pasta evenly. Serve immediately.

VEGETABLES

La verdura

Vegetables are the stars of the show in these recipes where the 20-minute cooking time maximises their freshness and flavour. I've even managed to include a vegetable tart using ready-made pastry for a handy shortcut and a quick vegetable risotto made with microwaveable rice, so you can still enjoy these dishes without wasting time with lots of stirring or baking. Ready-made polenta is also a great storecupboard staple and is a brilliant base for Italian-style vegetable dishes.

HONEY BEETROOT

with

BALSAMIC VINEGAR AND FETA

Fresh beetroot takes a long time to cook. However, in the chilled vegetable section of the supermarket you can find vacuum-packed cooked beetroot. It's a brilliant ingredient to use in quick recipes as the long, boring bit of the cooking has been done for you.

Barbabietola con miele e aceto balsamico

serves 4

3 x 250g packets of cooked beetroot
2 tablespoons extra virgin olive oil
2 tablespoons runny honey
A few sprigs of thyme
3 tablespoons balsamic vinegar
100g feta cheese
Salt and black pepper, to taste

1   Put a large frying pan over a high heat.

2   Remove the beetroot from the packet and quarter each one.

3   Add the oil to the pan and then the beetroot. Fry for 2 minutes before stirring in the honey and thyme. Cook for a further 2 minutes to allow the honey to caramelise.

4   Pour in the vinegar and deglaze the pan by stirring continuously with a wooden spoon.

5   Allow everything to bubble for 1 minute then spoon out into a serving bowl.

6   Crumble over the feta cheese, season to taste and serve.

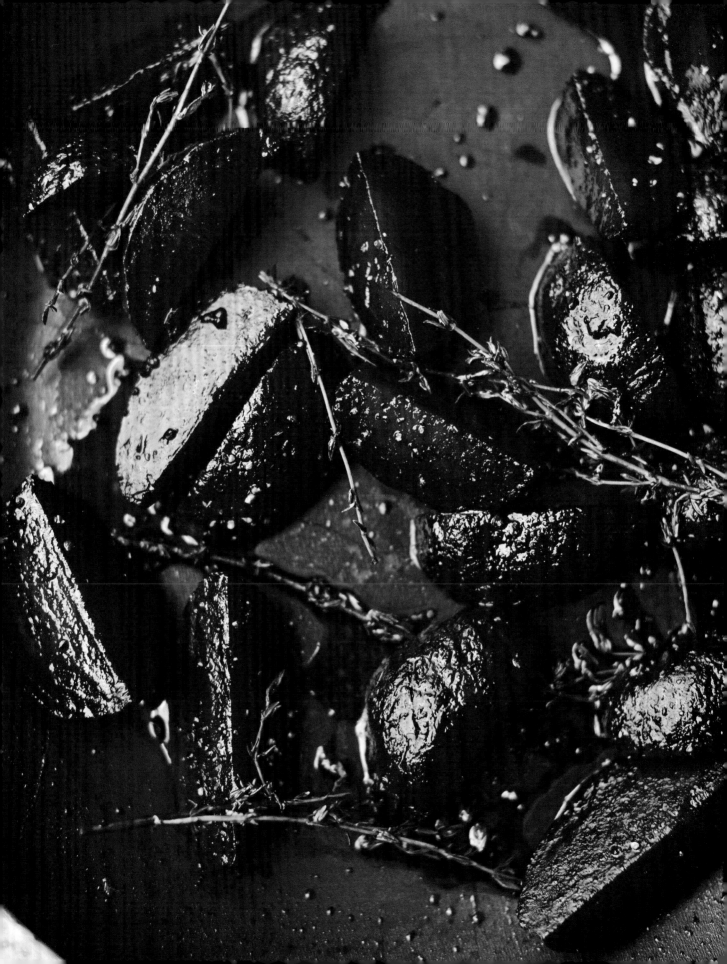

GRIDDLED AUBERGINES

with

TOMATOES AND HERB YOGURT

Vegetarian food can often lack texture and interest, but this dish is the complete opposite: soft aubergines, spicy tomato sauce and cooling yogurt, perfectly balanced by the texture of crunchy chickpeas. It makes a delicious vegetarian main course, but also works well as a side dish with a steak.

Melanzane grigliate

serves 4

3 large aubergines, cut into
1cm-thick rounds
6 tablespoons olive oil
1 garlic clove, peeled and sliced
Pinch of dried chilli flakes
400g cherry tomatoes, halved
1 teaspoon vegetable stock
powder
1 x 400g can chickpeas, drained
and rinsed
A few basil leaves, to garnish
Crusty bread, to serve
Salt and black pepper, to taste

for the herb yogurt:
250g Greek yogurt
1 garlic clove, peeled
Pinch of sugar
Small bunch of mixed soft herbs
(basil, parsley and chives all
work well)

1   Preheat the grill to moderate.

2   Put the aubergine rounds on a large baking tray. Drizzle with half the olive oil and season with salt and pepper. Pop the tray under the grill until the aubergines turn golden brown – this will take 2–4 minutes on each side.

3   While the aubergines are cooking on the first side, heat the remaining olive oil in a medium frying pan and add the garlic. Fry for 30 seconds, then add the chilli flakes and halved tomatoes. Cook for 2 minutes until the tomatoes start to release their juices.

4   Check the aubergines and if they are cooked and golden brown turn off the grill and leave them in the oven to keep warm.

5   Add 150ml water and the vegetable stock powder to the frying pan with the tomatoes and stir. Add the chickpeas and continue to cook over a low heat while you make the yogurt dressing. Stir occasionally.

6   Put the yogurt in a bowl and finely grate in the garlic. Season with a pinch of sugar, salt and pepper. Finally, chop the herbs and stir them into the yogurt.

7   Remove the aubergines from the oven and place them on a large platter. Spoon over the tomato and chickpeas, drizzle with the yogurt and scatter with a few fresh basil leaves. Serve with crusty bread.

BLUE CHEESE
and
ARTICHOKE DIP

Dips are a brilliant starter as they can be served from one or two bowls set in the middle of the table so that everybody can tuck in, which creates a great atmosphere. This dip combines the strong flavours of blue cheese and bitter walnuts with earthy artichokes. Sweet pears and crunchy radishes make ideal scoops.

Crema rustica di carciofi e Gorgonzola

serves 4

1 x 250g jar of artichoke hearts in oil, drained
100g mayonnaise
100g Gorgonzola cheese, cut into cubes
25g freshly grated Parmesan cheese
40g walnut halves, roughly chopped
1 ciabatta
2 tablespoons olive oil
2 pears
12 small radishes
Black pepper, to taste

1 Preheat the oven to 200°C/gas 6 and put a griddle pan over a high heat.

2 Roughly chop the artichokes and put in a ceramic baking dish with the mayonnaise, Gorgonzola and Parmesan.

3 Scatter over the walnuts. Season with a little black pepper and transfer the dish to the oven for 10 minutes to warm through. Stir after 5 minutes.

4 Meanwhile, cut the ciabatta into thin slices and brush with the olive oil. Put the slices on the griddle pan and cook for 1 minute on each side until crisp.

5 Cut the pears into quarters, remove the core and cut into thin slices. Arrange on a serving plate with the washed radishes.

6 Remove the dip from the oven and serve with the toasted ciabatta, sliced pear and radishes.

CREAMY PEA
and
SPINACH BRUSCHETTA

Who needs canned beans on toast when you can just as quickly rustle up this recipe? Peas are always in my freezer as my kids love them and they are super quick to cook and so good for you. In this recipe they are the star of the show rather than a side dish.

Bruschetta calda con spinaci

serves 2

1 ciabatta
2 tablespoons olive oil
400g bag of washed baby spinach leaves
2 garlic cloves, peeled, one left whole, one halved
250g frozen peas
50ml vegetable stock
100g mascarpone cheese
Small bunch of chives
50g Parmesan cheese
Salt and black pepper, to taste

1   Put a griddle pan and a frying pan over a high heat.

2   Cut 4 thick slices of ciabatta and brush on both sides with 1 tablespoon of the olive oil. Toast on the griddle pan for 2 minutes on each side until crisp. Set aside.

3   Pour 1 tablespoon of olive oil into the frying pan and add the spinach. Once it starts to wilt, use a fine grater to grate in 1 garlic clove. Cook for 1 minute before stirring in the frozen peas.

4   Pour in the stock, bring to a simmer then stir in the mascarpone. Once it has melted and the sauce is hot, use scissors to chop in the chives and then grate in the Parmesan. Finally season with black pepper and a little salt if needed. Set aside.

5   Rub the toasted bread with the remaining garlic clove.

6   Place 2 slices of toasted garlic bread on each plate and spoon over the pea and spinach mixture. Enjoy.

CRISPY MOZZARELLA SANDWICH

with

CRANBERRY SAUCE

Panini con mozzarella croccante

This is my take on the French classic, deep-fried Brie with cranberry sauce; it makes a great alternative to a boring cheese sandwich. It has all the right elements: warm gooey cheese, crispy toasted bread and cool crunchy lettuce.

serves 2

2 x 125g balls of cow's milk mozzarella
150g ready-made fine dried breadcrumbs
50g flour
2 eggs, beaten in a small bowl
2 small baguettes
4 tablespoons olive oil
3 tablespoons cranberry sauce
2 handfuls of mixed lettuce leaves
Salt and black pepper, to taste

1 Preheat the grill to moderate.

2 Rip each mozzarella ball into about 8 pieces.

3 Put the breadcrumbs on a plate and the flour on another. Season the flour with salt and pepper.

4 Dip the pieces of mozzarella in the flour, then in the beaten egg and then in the breadcrumbs. Pop each piece back into the egg and once more into the breadcrumbs. Set aside.

5 Cut the baguettes in half lengthways then place them cut-side up under the grill. Grill until golden brown.

6 Heat the olive oil in a frying pan and fry the mozzarella pieces for 3 minutes, turning frequently, to get the pieces crispy and brown all over. Place on kitchen paper to absorb any excess oil and set aside.

7 Remove the bread from under the grill and spread the cut sides with cranberry sauce. Place the crispy mozzarella onto the baguette, top with some salad leaves and cover with the other half of the baguette. Enjoy your sandwich!

VEGETABLE COUSCOUS

with

PESTO DRESSING

Couscous, like pasta, needs a helping hand with flavours and should be well seasoned. Making it with stock powder – far quicker than using a stock cube – adds a great base flavour and the pesto dressing gives this side dish an all-Italian twist.

Couscous al pesto

serves 6-8

300g couscous
2 teaspoons vegetable stock powder
4 tablespoons olive oil
1 aubergine, trimmed and cut into 2cm cubes
2 courgettes, trimmed and cut into 1cm rounds
1 x 280g jar of red and yellow peppers, drained and roughly chopped
A handful of pitted black olives
100g semi-dried tomatoes in oil, drained

for the pesto dressing:
Large bunch of basil
1 small garlic clove, peeled
30g pine nuts
150ml olive oil
50g freshly grated Parmesan cheese
Salt and black pepper, to taste

1 Fill and boil the kettle and put a frying pan over a high heat. Have a small blender ready for later.

2 Place the couscous in a large heatproof bowl, sprinkle in the stock powder and mix together. Pour in 500ml of boiling water, stir well, cover with clingfilm and set aside.

3 Pour the oil into the hot pan and fry the aubergines and courgettes for 8 minutes until golden brown; remove from the heat.

4 While the courgettes and aubergines cook, make the dressing. Put the basil into the blender with the garlic and pine nuts. Pour in half the olive oil and blend until smooth. Add the Parmesan and blend once more, adding in the rest of the oil to create a dressing. Season with salt and black pepper.

5 Use a fork to loosen the couscous grains, then stir in the chopped peppers, olives, semi-dried tomatoes, aubergines and courgettes.

6 Stir the pesto dressing into the couscous and spoon onto a large serving plate.

STUFFED FOCACCIA

In Italy you often get a beautiful basket of bread before the start of the meal to nibble on. In the south of Italy it is often rubbed with tomatoes and it is absolutely delicious. I dedicate my Panuozzo to my brother-in-law Orlando, because every time he comes to see me in London he always asks me to make it for him.

Panuozzo

serves 4

1 large focaccia
200g cherry tomatoes
150g green pitted olives in brine, drained
200g Taleggio cheese, sliced
200g rocket leaves

1 Preheat the grill to moderate.

2 Cut the focaccia in half horizontally. Place it on a baking tray, cut-side up, and grill for 5 minutes until lightly golden brown.

3 Remove the bread from under the grill. Now it's time to get messy. Cut the tomatoes in half then squeeze them in your hands over the bottom half of the toasted bread so that all the juices are soaked up and the crushed tomatoes remain on top.

4 Roughly chop the olives and scatter them over the tomatoes, then top with the slices of Taleggio.

5 Finally add the rocket leaves and top with the other piece of bread.

6 Place the giant sandwich back under the grill, on a slightly lower rack this time, and grill for 5 minutes. You want it to slowly go crispy and golden brown on the top so that the centre has a chance to warm through.

7 Remove from the oven, cut into four and serve with a cold Italian beer.

BAKED MUSHROOMS
ON TOAST

This is my take on mushrooms on toast and it makes a perfect midweek supper. It is easily adapted for the meat eaters in the family with a little bit of pancetta placed on top before cooking. You can always add a touch of paprika or cayenne if you like a spice kick. Italian Taleggio is a great cheese for cooking as it melts most satisfyingly.

Funghi al forno

serves 4

8 large flat field mushrooms, stalks removed
250g Taleggio cheese, cut into small cubes
8 sun-dried tomatoes in oil, drained then cut into strips
3 tablespoons olive oil
4 thick slices of sourdough bread
Salt and black pepper, to taste

For the side salad:
¼ cucumber
1 tablespoon wholegrain mustard
Pinch of caster sugar
2 tablespoons balsamic vinegar
4 tablespoons extra virgin olive oil
100g peppery green salad

1   Preheat the oven to 190°C/gas 5.

2   Put the mushrooms on a large baking tray, gills facing up.

3   Scatter the Taleggio cubes on top of the mushrooms. Top the cheese with the strips of tomatoes. Drizzle with the olive oil and season with salt and pepper.

4   Bake for 10 minutes until the cheese has melted and the mushrooms are soft.

5   Meanwhile, cut the cucumber into matchsticks and put in a large bowl.

6   Toast the sourdough bread.

7   Whisk together the mustard, caster sugar and balsamic vinegar in a small bowl. Slowly whisk in the extra virgin olive oil with 1 tablespoon of cold water. Season with salt and pepper.

8   Dress the salad leaves and cucumber with the dressing.

9   Place the toasted bread in the middle of each serving plate and top each slice with 2 mushrooms. Serve with the green salad.

GRIDDLED POLENTA

with

WILD MUSHROOM RAGÙ

Mushrooms are a great base for a vegetarian meal even if you are a meat eater. They have a naturally meaty texture and are very filling, so even the most avid carnivore won't miss the steak! Italians love wild mushrooms and I'm no exception. Try this creamy ragù for a simple midweek supper.

Polenta alla griglia con ragù di funghi

serves 4

25g salted butter
3 tablespoons olive oil
450g chestnut mushrooms, sliced
150g button mushrooms, halved
250g mixed wild mushrooms,
roughly chopped
1 garlic clove, peeled
1 tablespoon plain flour
A good splash of white wine
300ml hot vegetable stock
300ml double cream
500g block of ready-made polenta
1 tablespoon freshly chopped
tarragon
Parmesan shavings, to serve
Salt and pepper, to taste

1 Preheat a griddle pan.

2 Heat the butter and 1 tablespoon of oil in a large frying pan and when melted add the mushrooms. Try not to move them around too much as this will allow them to take on some colour. Once lightly golden brown, grate in the garlic. Cook for 30 seconds before adding the flour. Stir well before pouring in the white wine. Bring to the boil, then pour in the stock and cream.

3 Stir everything together and allow to simmer for 5 minutes. Stir occasionally with a wooden spoon.

4 While the mushrooms cook, slice the polenta into 12 slices. Brush both sides with the remaining olive oil then place on the hot griddle for 1 minute on each side.

5 Stir the tarragon through the mushroom ragù and season well with salt and pepper.

6 Arrange the griddled polenta on 4 serving plates, spoon over the creamy mushroom ragù and top with some Parmesan shavings.

BAKED POLENTA
with
TOMATO AND RED PEPPER SAUCE

The ready-made blocks of polenta that you can now buy in the supermarket are great for a quick supper. Half the work is already done for you and there is no need to boil, whisk, cool and set it. I often have a packet in my kitchen for when I just don't feel like any other form of carbohydrate or for when I just feel like something a bit different.

Polenta al forno con peperoni rossi

serves 2

**3 tablespoons olive oil, plus
a little extra for brushing
1 x 290g jar of roasted red
peppers in brine or oil, drained
and sliced
2 medium courgettes, cut into
1cm cubes
1 garlic clove, peeled and sliced
Pinch of dried chilli flakes
1 x 400g can cherry tomatoes
100g pitted black olives in brine,
drained
500g block of ready-made polenta
1 x 125g ball of mozzarella,
drained
25g fresh breadcrumbs
10 basil leaves
Salt and white pepper, to taste**

1   Preheat the grill to moderate.

2   Heat the olive oil in a medium frying pan and fry the peppers and courgettes for 1 minute. Stir with a wooden spoon.

3   Add the garlic and chilli and continue to fry for a further minute.

4   Pour in the tomatoes, add the olives and simmer for 5 minutes, uncovered. Stir occasionally.

5   Put a second frying pan over a medium heat.

6   Slice the block of polenta into 1cm thick slices, brush both sides with a little olive oil and fry in the preheated frying pan for 1 minute on each side. Arrange the polenta in a small ovenproof dish so that the slices are just overlapping.

7   Tear the mozzarella into pieces and set aside.

8   Season the tomato and pepper sauce with salt and pepper. Spoon it over the polenta and scatter over the mozzarella.

9   Sprinkle the fresh breadcrumbs and basil leaves on top and drizzle with a little more olive oil. Season with salt and pepper. Put under the grill for 2 minutes or until the cheese has melted and the breadcrumbs are crispy. Serve hot.

NEW POTATO SALAD
with
RED ONIONS AND CAPERS

Adding just-boiled new potatoes into a dressing means they absorb all the flavours as they cool; it is as if they open up and suck in all the flavour. Italians use a lot of red onions, which are much milder than white or yellow ones – perfect for salads – and capers add a lemony tang. This recipe couldn't be easier, and is a great little trick to have up your sleeve.

Patate e cipolle rosse

serves 6

800g baby new potatoes, washed
1 medium red onion, peeled and sliced
2 tablespoons capers in brine, washed and drained
6 tablespoons extra virgin olive oil
Juice of 1 lemon
100g pitted green olives, drained and halved
3 tablespoons freshly chopped chives
Salt and black pepper, to taste

1 Fill a large saucepan with boiling water from the kettle and put over a high heat. Add a good pinch of salt and the potatoes. Boil for 10 minutes or until tender.

2 Meanwhile, put the onion in a large bowl with the capers, extra virgin olive oil and lemon juice. Mix everything together and set aside.

3 Add the olives to the bowl.

4 When the potatoes are tender, drain them and pop them straight into the bowl with the dressing. Add in the chives, season with salt and pepper and stir all together.

5 Serve warm to accompany any of your favourite dishes.

QUICK RISOTTO

with

LEMON, PEAS AND PARMESAN

Risotto is one of my favourite meals to eat, but sometimes I don't have the time to stand and stir for 20 minutes. This is my speedy version; its beautiful creaminess comes from the mascarpone and a good helping of Parmesan cheese.

Risotto veloce con limone e piselli

---

serves 4

4 tablespoons olive oil
4 spring onions, finely sliced
2 x 200g packets of microwaveable packet rice
1 tablespoon vegetable stock powder
100ml hot water
200g frozen peas, defrosted
Grated zest of 1 unwaxed lemon
4 tablespoons mascarpone cheese
60g freshly grated Parmesan cheese
Salt and white pepper, to taste

To serve:
3 tablespoons freshly chopped flatleaf parsley
150g pea shoots
Parmesan cheese
Extra virgin olive oil, to drizzle

1 Heat the olive oil in a medium saucepan.

2 Fry the spring onions in the hot oil for 2 minutes. Stir occasionally with a wooden spoon.

3 Stir in the packets of rice (no need to microwave them first) then add the stock powder and water. Stir well, breaking up the rice with the wooden spoon. Cook for 2 minutes.

4 Add the peas and cook for a further 2 minutes. Continue to stir with the wooden spoon.

5 Reduce the heat and add the lemon zest and mascarpone cheese. Sprinkle over the grated Parmesan and season with salt and pepper. Stir all together.

6 Spoon onto 4 warm serving plates, top with the fresh parsley and a handful of pea shoots then use a speed peeler to create shavings of Parmesan on top. Finish with a drizzle of extra virgin olive oil.

SUMMER VEGETABLE TART

This is a beautifully simple summer tart. The pastry is cooked blind while you make the filling so it is super quick to prepare. If you have a couple of courgettes in the fridge, or some fresh herbs, add them to the sautéed vegetables; you can make this dish up as you go along.

Tartina di asparagi

serves 4

1 sheet of ready-made rolled puff pastry
150g spring onions
1 tablespoon olive oil
150g fine asparagus spears, trimmed
100g frozen peas, defrosted
100ml crème fraîche
100g mascarpone cheese
50g freshly grated Parmesan cheese
50g rocket leaves
2 tablespoons extra virgin olive oil
Salt and black pepper, to taste

1 Preheat the oven to 200°C/gas 6.

2 Unroll the pastry and place on a non-stick baking tray. Use the point of a sharp knife to mark a border 2cm from the edge all the way round the sheet, taking care not to go all the way through. Use a fork to gently prick the pastry inside the border; this will stop it rising too much. Bake the pastry in the oven for 12 minutes.

3 Meanwhile, trim the spring onions to the same length as the asparagus spears. Heat the olive oil in a frying pan and fry the spring onions and asparagus for 1 minute.

4 Place the peas in a bowl and pour over 50ml boiling water from a kettle. Give them a quick stir and then set aside for 2 minutes, until the water has evaporated. Season with salt and pepper.

5 Mix together the crème fraîche, mascarpone and Parmesan in a large bowl. Season with a little salt and pepper.

6 Once the pastry is golden brown and risen, remove it from the oven and use a clean tea-towel to push down the puffed up central area of pastry so that you are left with a clear and defined border.

7 Spoon the cheese mixture over the central area of the pastry and spread out with a palette knife. Scatter over the cooked vegetables and top with the rocket leaves. Finish with a drizzle of extra virgin olive oil and a little salt and black pepper. Serve hot.

DESSERTS

I dolci

Pudding can often be an afterthought, particularly for everyday meals, so here are some ideas to quickly satisfy any after-dinner sweet cravings. From a simple fruit sorbet to a speedy chocolate pudding that you can whip up in the microwave, it's possible to make a range of dishes with only a little time. There's no need to wait for anything to cook or set so you can indulge in these delicious treats straight away.

FROZEN FRUITS SORBET

with

LIMONCELLO

This has to be the easiest and quickest recipe in the book. I have actually made this in less than 5 minutes and yet no one believed it. The taste is incredible and it can be counted towards your five a day – win, win!

Sorbetto tutti frutti

serves 4

500g mixed frozen fruits (blueberries, raspberries, strawberries, mangoes)
80g icing sugar
2 tablespoons limoncello liqueur, cold

1   Put the frozen fruits and the icing sugar in a food processor. Pour over the limoncello and blitz for about 2 minutes until smooth. It may need another blast to break up the frozen fruits.

2   Spoon the Sorbetto Tutti Frutti into dessert glasses and serve immediately. Alternatively, you can freeze the sorbet in a plastic sealed container for up to 2 months.

STRAWBERRIES AND ALMONDS

with

AMARETTO LIQUEUR AND GREEK YOGURT

Strawberries are on sale in supermarkets all year round but more often than not, the flavour isn't good unless they are in season. This recipe is perfect for those months when the berries are lacking their full taste and sweetness, as the Amaretto and honey add that extra something the fruit needs. This is a lovely refreshing dessert that will look really impressive if served in cocktail glasses.

Fragole, Amaretto e mandorle

serves 4

800g strawberries
3 tablespoons Amaretto liqueur
2 tablespoons runny honey
300g plain Greek yogurt
4 tablespoons flaked almonds
4 fresh mint leaves, to decorate

1   Wash the strawberries under cold water, drain and pat dry with kitchen paper.

2   Remove and discard the green stalks and cut the strawberries in half. Place in a large bowl.

3   Pour in the Amaretto liqueur and drizzle over the honey.

4   Mix well and leave to marinate for 10 minutes at room temperature. Stir occasionally.

5   Divide the yogurt between 4 dessert glasses and spoon over the marinated strawberries.

6   Drizzle with the remaining juices from the marinade and scatter over the flaked almonds. Top each glass with a fresh mint leaf.

SUMMER BERRIES

with

WHITE CHOCOLATE SAUCE

During the summer my fridge is always filled with a variety of berries for the kids to nibble on when they are hungry. This is the most simple of desserts with ingredients that are usually in the cupboard or fridge. It's a crowd-pleaser for adults and kids alike.

Frutta d'estate con cioccolata bianca

serves 6

200g good-quality white chocolate, broken into small pieces
50ml double cream
50g flaked almonds
3 tablespoons icing sugar
750g chilled summer berries (raspberries, strawberries or blueberries)
2 tablespoons crème fraîche

1 Put the chocolate pieces and the cream in a heatproof bowl. Set the bowl over a saucepan of just simmering water and allow to gently melt.

2 Meanwhile, heat a frying pan over a high heat and get a piece of baking paper out on the work surface.

3 Put the flaked almonds into the pan and dust with the icing sugar. Stir them constantly over a high heat for 1–2 minutes until they start to turn golden brown. Once lightly golden and caramelised, tip them out onto the baking paper to cool.

4 Divide the berries between 6 glasses or bowls.

5 Once the chocolate has melted, remove the bowl from the heat and stir in the crème fraîche. Spoon the sauce over the berries and scatter with the caramelised almonds.

6 Serve immediately while the sauce is still hot.

THIN PANCAKES

with

FRESHLY SQUEEZED LEMON JUICE

Say 'pancakes' in our house and everyone associates it with Saturday mornings when chocolate and banana pancakes are my speciality. I didn't really serve them as desserts after a meal until recently and now I can't understand why I didn't. If you are having fish or a light meal, this is a perfect dessert, now firmly on my top ten list. The flavours really round off your meal perfectly.

Crespelle al limone

serves 4

100g plain white flour
Pinch of salt
1 large egg
300ml full-fat milk
Zest of 1 unwaxed lemon
2 teaspoons sunflower oil
Juice of 2 lemons
1 tablespoon caster sugar
4 tablespoons Cointreau
300g strawberries, hulled and sliced

1 Sift the flour and salt into a large mixing bowl. Add the egg, milk and lemon zest and whisk together until smooth.

2 Heat a small, heavy-based frying pan over a medium heat. Add a few drops of oil and rub it over the base to allow it to heat. Pour in an eighth of the batter and tilt the pan so that the mixture spreads evenly over the base to make a thin pancake.

3 As soon as the pancake has set and bubbles appear on the surface, flip it over to cook the other side. Repeat the process to make 8 pancakes in total, transferring them to kitchen paper as you cook them. Once all the pancakes are cooked, fold them into triangles.

4 Wipe the frying pan clean with a piece of kitchen paper. Pour in the lemon juice and add the sugar. Heat gently to dissolve the sugar then pour in the Cointreau.

5 Return all the pancakes to the frying pan, overlapping them to fit. Cook gently for 30 seconds.

6 Serve 2 pancakes per person with slices of strawberries scattered over the top.

CAPPUCCINO MOUSSE

I love my coffee; it's the first thing I have in the morning and I keep my cup topped up during the day. So this dessert is for those of you who, like me, also enjoy a hit of coffee at the end of the day too.

Cappuccino mousse

Makes 4 large or 6 small

150g marshmallows
50g salted butter
50g caster sugar
250g dark chocolate (approx. 70 per cent cocoa solids), finely chopped
60ml espresso coffee
300ml double cream

for the topping:
8 tablespoons crème fraîche
1 tablespoon icing sugar
1 teaspoon vanilla bean paste
Chocolate-covered coffee beans, to decorate
Cocoa powder or finely grated chocolate, to dust

1 Place the marshmallows, butter, sugar, chocolate and espresso in a small saucepan and warm slowly until melted.

2 Meanwhile, whip the cream to medium/firm peaks.

3 Remove the melted chocolate and marshmallow mixture from the heat and pour into a large bowl. Stir gently until cooled to room temperature and then fold in the cream.

4 Spoon the mixture into 4 or 6 glasses.

5 Mix together the crème fraîche, icing sugar and vanilla then spoon on top of the coffee chocolate mousse.

6 Scatter with a few chocolate-covered coffee beans, dust lightly with cocoa powder or grated chocolate, and serve.

SUPERFAST CHOCOLATE PUDDING

You might not believe me if I told you you could cook a chocolate pudding in just sixty seconds, but it's true!

Tortino al cioccolato velocissimo

serves 4

Butter, for greasing
4 tablespoons Nutella
6 tablespoons full-fat milk
12 tablespoons self-raising flour
5 tablespoons caster sugar
1 tablespoon cocoa powder
2 medium eggs
2 tablespoons sunflower oil
3 tablespoons Amaretto liqueur
100g white chocolate, cut into small pieces
Vanilla ice cream, to serve

1 Grease 4 coffee mugs with butter.

2 Put the Nutella in a small bowl and pour over 4 tablespoons of the milk. Mix and divide between the 4 coffee mugs. Set aside.

3 Put the flour, sugar and cocoa powder in a large bowl. Crack in the eggs and pour over the oil, the remaining milk and the Amaretto liqueur. Mix well with a wooden spoon to create a smooth paste. Fold in the small pieces of white chocolate.

4 Divide the mixture equally and neatly between the coffee mugs.

5 Microwave each mug, one at a time, on full power (1000W) for 1 minute.

6 Turn out the chocolate puddings on to a plate and serve with a ball of ice cream on top.

HOT CHOCOLATE ORANGE FONDUE

This is a great one for the kids. It takes more time to eat it than it does to make and they will be kept busy creating their own combinations on skewers ready for dunking.

Fonduta di cioccolato

serves 8

400g dark chocolate (approx. 70 per cent cocoa solids), broken into small pieces
85g salted butter
300ml double cream
300ml full-fat milk
Zest of 2 oranges
2 tablespoons orange liqueur (omit if making for children)

for dunking:
Strawberries
Marshmallows
Amaretti biscuits
Shop-bought sponge cake (chocolate or Madeira), cut into 2cm dice
Brazil nuts
Ready-prepared pineapple chunks
Blueberries

Wooden or metal skewers

1 Heat the chocolate, butter, cream and milk in a saucepan over a low heat. Warm gently until the chocolate has melted.

2 Meanwhile, prepare the tasty treats for dunking on a board or large plate.

3 Stir the orange zest and liqueur (if using) into the melted chocolate – if the chocolate seizes (becomes stiff and unwieldy) at this stage, add 1 tablespoon of boiling water and stir until it is once again smooth and melted.

4 Pour the chocolate fondue into a fondue pot or place the saucepan on the board alongside the fruit and other bits.

5 Don't forget the skewers for dunking, otherwise it's going to get messy!

CHOCOLATE AND CHERRY TRIFLES

I am a firm believer of 'fresh is best' but when cherries are out of season or when you just don't have the time to remove their stones, canned ones sold in their natural juice are perfect. The juices are used in this recipe to moisten the sponge, adding yet more flavour.

Zuppetta Inglese

serves 4

**190g dark chocolate (approx.
70 per cent cocoa solids)
150ml double cream
250ml ready-made custard
175g mascarpone
250g Madeira or chocolate
sponge cake
1 x 425g can pitted cherries
in natural juice, 4 reserved for
decoration
4 tablespoons Amaretto liqueur**

1 Break up 150g of the chocolate into small pieces and put in a heatproof bowl set over a saucepan of just simmering water. As soon as it has melted, remove the bowl from the heat and set aside.

2 Pour the cream into a separate bowl, whip to soft peaks and set aside.

3 Mix together the custard and mascarpone in a third bowl.

4 Cut the sponge into 1cm cubes and place a layer in the base of 4 straight-sided glasses. Spoon over some of the canned cherries, along with their juices, and add 1 tablespoon of Amaretto to each glass.

5 Stir the cooled melted chocolate through the custard.

6 Spoon half the custard mixture over the soaked sponge and cherries. Top with a little more sponge and some more cherries, then finish with the remaining custard mix.

7 Top with a spoonful of whipped cream and place a cherry on top.

8 Grate the remaining chocolate over the top and serve.

ZABAGLIONE

with

MARSALA WINE

What a fantastic, easy, classic Italian dessert. Who would think you could create something so delicious with three ingredients? It looks fantastic when served and always tastes amazing. Do be careful when warming the egg yolks over the pan of simmering water: the bowl must not touch the water and the water must be simmering not boiling. This recipe is not at all tricky but those rules are a must.

Zabaglione

serves 4

5 large eggs
250ml Marsala wine
80g caster sugar

1 Break the eggs into a small bowl and use your fingertips to lift up the egg yolks and place them in a large heatproof glass bowl. (Cover the egg whites with clingfilm and keep in the fridge for the next time you decide to make a meringue.)

2 Pour the Marsala wine into a medium saucepan and simmer gently until reduced by half. Leave to cool then stir in 20g of the sugar.

3 Put the remaining sugar in the bowl with the egg yolks and beat with an electric whisk for 5 minutes until thick and pale yellow.

4 Set the bowl over a saucepan of just simmering water (make sure the water is not in contact with the bowl) and continue to whisk for a further 10 minutes, gradually drizzling in the Marsala wine.

5 The egg mixture should almost triple in volume and have a light, foamy texture and be able to hold soft peaks when you lift the whisk. Make sure that the egg mixture doesn't become too hot or it will start to cook around the edges of the bowl – resulting in sweet scrambled egg!

6 Spoon the zabaglione into 4 tall glasses and serve immediately.

Index